MOORE COUNTY HORSE COUNTRY *Cooking*

Copyright © 2014 by Victory 500 Marketing

ISBN: 978-0-9722366-7-6
First Edition

All rights reserved. No part of this book may be reproduced or transmitted in any form or by any means, electronic or mechanical, including photocopying, recording, or by any information storage and retrieval system without the written permission of the publisher, except where permitted by law.
Printed in Canada.

Publisher: Kathy Virtue
Marketing Manager: Leigh Virtue
Layout & Design: Scott Yancey and Brad Beard
Editors: Greg Girard and Amanda Jakl
Intern: Grace Vermeulen

Front cover photo courtesy of Moore County Hounds.
Back cover photo courtesy of Landon Russell.

Foreword
by Katie Walsh

Many thanks and blessings go to the Virtue family, and all those wonderful people in the horse community who contributed recipes and pictures for this cookbook.

Proceeds will benefit The Walthour-Moss Foundation, a 501(c)(3) public charity, whose mission is to preserve open land, to protect and improve wildlife habitat, and to provide a place for equestrian purposes.

The Walthour-Moss Foundation is the only nature preserve in the state, and one of the few in the country with a stated mission designating it as a place for equestrian activity. Open year round, sunrise to sunset, the foundation provides miles of quiet trails and sandy lanes for equestrian use. It's in the very heart of Moore County horse country, and a regional destination for equestrians from more than 45 North Carolina counties as well as nearby Virginia and South Carolina.

Declared a "Significant Natural Heritage Area" by the North Carolina Natural Heritage Program, the foundation is home to more than 650 plant species and more than 31 documented rare or threatened species of flora and fauna, and has the largest pond cypress in America.

In 2013, the U.S. Department of the Interior placed more than 2,500 acres of the 4,092 acres under stewardship of the Walthour-Moss Foundation on the National Register of Historic Places. The North Carolina State Historic Preservation Office and the U.S. Department of the Interior deemed the property to be of state and national significance due to its long history of conservation and the integrity of the landscape.

Photo: Courtesy of Moore County Historical Association Collection, Southern Pines, NC

Contents

Appetizers
6

Soups & Salads
20

Sides
40

Entrées
58

Desserts
88

Breads, Breakfast & Beverages
126

Horse Show Tailgating
140

Appetizers

Photo: Courtesy of Moore County Historical Association Collection, Southern Pines, NC

Photo: Courtesy of Mary Strasser

Caviar Pie
Contributed by Lee Sedwick

INGREDIENTS | SERVES 12
- ½ pint guacamole
- 12 eggs
- 1 sweet onion, chopped and divided
- Mayonnaise to taste (optional)
- 2 jars (4 ounces each) domestic or Norwegian caviar
- Anchovies (optional)

DIRECTIONS
Hard boil eggs and let cool. Dice eggs and add half chopped onion. Add mayonnaise to taste and texture for spreading.

In serving dish, spread guacamole. Layer egg mixture on top, then top with layer of caviar in an artistic pattern.

May add anchovies for decoration. Top with remaining chopped onion.

Serve on small, crustless bread squares.

Olé Olé
Contributed by Mary Strasser

INGREDIENTS
- 8 ounces cream cheese
- 1 can (15 ounces) chili without beans
- 1 cup chopped green onion
- 1 can (4 ounces) sliced ripe olives
- 1 cup shredded Monterey Jack cheese

DIRECTIONS
Preheat oven to 325 F.

Using 9-by-1-inch pie plate, layer ingredients in the order listed.

Bake 25 minutes.

Serve with taco chips.

Photo: Courtesy of Landon Russell

Hot Cheese Rounds

Contributed by Danielle Veasy

INGREDIENTS | YIELDS 36-48

1 can (4.25 ounces) chopped black olives
2 cups sharp cheddar cheese, grated
2-3 tablespoons minced onion
1 cup mayonnaise
1 package (1 pound) party cocktail bread, sliced

DIRECTIONS

Preheat oven to 350 F.

In bowl, mix black olives, cheese, onion and mayonnaise. Spread a tablespoon of mixture onto party cocktail bread slice. Bake on cookie sheet 15 minutes or until bubbly.

May also be frozen on a cookie sheet, then transferred to a plastic bag or covered container. Thaw slightly before baking or reheating.

Baked Brie

Contributed by Tara Butler

INGREDIENTS | SERVES 12-16

1 round (8 ounces) Brie
¼ cup chopped pecans
¼ cup brown sugar
2 tablespoons brandy

DIRECTIONS

Preheat oven to 400 F.

Bake brie 5 minutes, until soft.

Combine pecans, sugar, brandy, and place on top of brie.

Bake another 5-7 minutes until topping is melted.

Photo: Courtesy of Jim Secky

Uncle Jim's Famous Water Chestnuts and Bacon

Contributed by Jim Secky

INGREDIENTS

2 pounds bacon with straight edges
1 box (1 pound) dark brown sugar
4 cans (8 ounces each) whole water chestnuts
¼ cup butter
1 bottle (12 ounces) dark brown mustard
4 (9 inches) disposable aluminum pie pans
1 pack (250 count) round wooden toothpicks

DIRECTIONS

Preheat oven to 450 F.

Lay out a sheet of foil. Cut bacon in half and lay strips out next to each other. Sprinkle brown sugar generously on each strip.

Roll one whole chestnut in each strip of bacon and pin with a toothpick. Place batch in buttered pie plate and cook until bacon is completely done, about 10 minutes. Sugar may burn a bit if cooked too long.

Unload pans while bacon is still hot. Dab grease off with paper towel before putting in oven-proof dish to reheat before serving.

Pour off extra grease from used tins and dribble melted sugar over pieces in serving dish.

Serve with mustard dipping sauce. Can be enjoyed cold as well.

The late Ida Zaninni of Providence, Rhode Island, gave this recipe to us in 1974. In the last 40 years, I've made at least 10,000 of these great appetizers and can't remember any leftovers. The photo is our horse Griffin who's as happy as can be.

Photo: Courtesy of Moore County Hounds

Bacon Wrapped Crackers

Contributed by Wayne Moore

INGREDIENTS
1 sleeve butter crackers
8 ounces Parmesan cheese
1 pound thick sliced bacon, cut in half

DIRECTIONS
Preheat oven to 200 F.

Spread crackers on 9-by-13-inch baking sheet and sprinkle with cheese.

Wrap each cracker with half piece of bacon. Bake 2 hours. Top with more cheese just before removing from oven.

Damian and Jose's Oysters Argentina

Contributed by Cameron Sadler

INGREDIENTS
1 teaspoon chopped parsley
1 teaspoon minced garlic
½ teaspoon freshly ground pepper
½ cup white wine, champagne, or coconut milk
2 tablespoons Parmesan cheese
24 oysters in the half shell

DIRECTIONS
Preheat oven to 350 F.

Sprinkle ingredients over oysters in the half shell and bake 5 minutes or until oysters have curled.

Photo: Courtesy of Sgt. Major Kevin Riley

Cranberry Cheese Ball

Contributed by Nancy Moore

INGREDIENTS | SERVES 12-16

8 ounces regular cream cheese, softened
4 - 4.5 ounces blue cheese
3 - 4.5 ounces soft spreading Port wine cheddar cheese, softened
6-8 ounces dried cranberries, divided

DIRECTIONS

In mixer, blend cheeses. Add cranberries. Make into ball and refrigerate, uncovered, until firm.

Cover outside with remaining dried cranberries and serve. Refrigerate covered until ready to eat.

Guacamole

Contributed by Sassy Riley

INGREDIENTS

3-4 ripe avocados
1 lemon, juiced
Salt and pepper to taste
Minced onion to taste
Red pepper to taste

DIRECTIONS

Mash avocados and combine with other ingredients.

Add minced jalapenos or cilantro, if desired.

Black Bean Salsa

Contributed by Anne Strobel

INGREDIENTS

- ¼ cup vegetable oil
- ¼ cup red wine vinegar
- ⅓ - ½ cup orange juice
- ¼ teaspoon salt
- 2 cans (15 ounces each) black beans, rinsed and drained
- 1 can (29 ounces) mandarin oranges, drained
- ½ small red onion, chopped
- 1 cup frozen corn, thawed
- 1 tablespoon chopped pickled jalapeno pepper

DIRECTIONS

In bowl, whisk oil, vinegar, orange juice and salt. Pour dressing over beans, oranges, onion, corn and pepper.

Toss and refrigerate until ready to serve. Serve with chips.

Red Dip Salsa

Contributed by Joan Baldwin

INGREDIENTS

- 1 can (10 ounces) tomato sauce with bits
- ¼ teaspoon crushed red pepper flakes
- ¼ teaspoon garlic salt
- 1 teaspoon ground cumin

DIRECTIONS

Mix well and enjoy.

Photo: Courtesy of Caroline Young

Baked Clams

Contributed by Stephen Later

INGREDIENTS

¼ cup water
3 slices bacon, cut into cubes
½ pound mushrooms, minced
1 ½ tablespoons finely chopped shallots or scallions
⅛ pound (2 ounces) Gruyere or Swiss cheese, cubed small
½ cup grated Parmesan or Romano cheese
2 tablespoons finely chopped parsley
1 clove garlic, minced
¾ cup fine soft breadcrumbs
½ cup minced celery
3 tablespoons dry white wine
1 egg yolk
Salt and pepper to taste
2 dozen cherrystone or littleneck clams

DIRECTIONS

Preheat oven to 400 F.

In large saucepan over medium heat, cook bacon until brown and crisp. Set aside. Pour off all but 2 tablespoons of fat from pan.

Add mushrooms and shallots. Cook until mushrooms sweat. Cool.

In medium bowl, mix cheeses, parsley, garlic, breadcrumbs, celery, wine and egg yolk. Add salt and pepper. Scoop over clam in half shell and bake 10 minutes.

Roasted Shrimp and Guacamole

Contributed by Mary Ellen Bailey

INGREDIENTS

2 pounds (12 to 15 count) large shrimp, peeled and deveined
½ teaspoon salt and pepper, to taste
1 tablespoon olive oil
1 tablespoon balsamic vinegar
1 jar (11.5 ounces) guacamole dip
Salt and pepper to taste

DIRECTIONS

Preheat oven to 350 F.

Salt and pepper shrimp. Toss with olive oil and balsamic vinegar. Spread shrimp on baking sheet.

Bake until shrimp are done. Serve immediately with guacamole for dipping.

The shrimp have a very different taste when cooked this way. Super easy and everyone will love it. The guacamole is a twist for dipping!

Photo: Courtesy of Pam Jensen

Photo: Courtesy of Moore County Historical Association Collection, Southern Pines, NC

Easy Crab Dip

Contributed by Aggie Cohen

INGREDIENTS

- 1 package (8 ounces) cream cheese
- 1 can (6.5 ounces) crab claw meat
- 1 bottle (11.5 ounces) cocktail sauce
- 1 box (9.5 ounces) whole grain wheat crackers

DIRECTIONS

Place cream cheese on a plate and cover with crabmeat. Then cover with cocktail sauce.

Surround with crackers. Stand back while guests stampede.

This recipe isn't fancy, but it is my go-to for last minute entertaining, and is always popular.

Yummy Chicken Dip

Contributed by Bri R. Gindlesperger

INGREDIENTS

- 1 pound skinless chicken breasts, cooked and shredded
- 16 ounces cream cheese, room temperature
- 1 cup ranch dressing
- 2 cups shredded cheddar cheese
- ¾ cups hot sauce

DIRECTIONS

Preheat oven to 350 F.

In medium bowl, combine cheeses, hot sauce and ranch dressing. Mix in shredded chicken.

Bake 20 minutes. Serve with chips.

Photo: Courtesy of Effie Ellis

Party Pizza Rounds
Contributed by Danielle Veasy

INGREDIENTS | YIELDS 4-6 dozen
- 1 pound ground beef
- 1 pound hot pork sausage or Italian sausage
- ½ teaspoon oregano
- ½ teaspoon onion or garlic powder
- 1 pound pasteurized processed cheese
- 2 packages (1 pound each) party cocktail bread (rye, onion or your favorite)

DIRECTIONS
Preheat oven to 350 F.

Remove casings from sausage and cook beef and sausage over medium-high until well cooked. Drain. Add oregano and onion or garlic powder, and mix well. Cut cheese into small chucks; add to meat mixture and heat until melted.

Spread mixture on party cocktail bread. Place on baking sheet; broil until brown and hot all the way through, about 10 minutes.

May also be frozen on a cookie sheet, then transferred to a plastic bag or covered container. Thaw slightly before cooking or reheating.

Empanadas Panamanian Canapé
Contributed by Mickey Wirtz

INGREDIENTS
- 1 large onion, chopped
- ½ cup stuffed olives
- ¼ cup sweet pickle
- 1 egg, hard-boiled, chopped
- ½ pound ground pork
- ½ cup raisins
- ¼ pound butter
- Salt and pepper to taste
- 2 packs (13 ounces each) dough for pastries

DIRECTIONS
Preheat oven to 350 F.

In medium bowl, mix onion, olives, pickles and egg. Mix with pork and raisins. In frying pan over medium-low heat, brown mixture in butter.

Roll pastry dough ⅛-inch thick and cut into rounds.

Place 1 tablespoon of meat mixture on pastry circle and fold over. Trim edges and prick with fork.

Bake 15 minutes on lightly-greased baking sheet.

Photo: Courtesy of Landon Russell

16 | MOORE COUNTY HORSE COUNTRY COOKING

Photo: Courtesy of Moore County Historical Association Collection, Southern Pines, NC

Emeline Harvey's Swedish Meatballs

Contributed by Lynn Harvey

INGREDIENTS | YIELDS 80, 1-inch balls

4 slices bread
¾ cup milk
1 pound round steak
½ pound lean pork
1 pound veal
1 onion, shredded
2 teaspoons salt
⅛ teaspoon ground nutmeg
1 clove garlic, mashed fine
¼ teaspoon black pepper
2 eggs, lightly beaten
Oil for frying
2 cups beef bouillon

DIRECTIONS

Preheat oven to 350 F.

In bowl, crumble bread and add milk. Blend until a paste-like consistency is reached. Add meat, seasoning and eggs. Beat and stir with wooden spoon until mixture is well blended.

Dip out with rounded teaspoon, and roll into 1-inch balls. Set on waxed paper, about ½ hour, to dry. Then, in a heavy skillet over medium heat, brown meatballs in ½-inch of oil.

Place browned meatballs in single layer onto a 9-by-13-inch baking pan. Add hot bouillon. Bake about 30 minutes, or until broth is absorbed.

Serve without gravy or sauce, or make gravy using 3 tablespoons oil, 4 tablespoons flour and enough water for desired consistency.

We used to have these on Christmas Eve at family reunions every year.

MOORE COUNTY HORSE COUNTRY COOKING | 17

Photo: Courtesy of Landon Russell

Betty Maness' Bourbon Hot Dogs

Contributed by Abby Shultis

INGREDIENTS | SERVES 30-40

¾ cup bourbon
½ cup ketchup
½ cup brown sugar
½ teaspoon oregano
1-2 tablespoons chopped onion
½ teaspoon rosemary
4 packages (14 ounces each) small hot dogs

DIRECTIONS

In small saucepan, mix bourbon, ketchup, sugar, oregano, onion and rosemary. Simmer on low for 1 hour.

Add hot dogs and simmer for an additional 15-20 minutes (use small hot dogs or cut up standard size). Serve in chafing dish over heat with toothpicks nearby.

This recipe came from Betty Maness, whose husband, William H., was born in Carthage. They lived in Jacksonville, Florida, where he was a well-known judge. Through my Sweet Briar College friendship with their daughter, Judy, they became surrogate parents during my first five years after graduation.

Irene's Opening Meet Sausage Balls

Contributed by Irene Russell

INGREDIENTS

1 pound hot sausage
1 cup shredded extra sharp cheddar cheese
2 cups Bisquick® mix

DIRECTIONS

Preheat oven to 400 F.

Combine ingredients thoroughly, by hand or with mixer. Roll into small balls and place on ungreased baking sheet. Bake 10-12 minutes until golden. Serve hot.

Can be made ahead of time and frozen.

Danny Robert Shaw winning Championship at Mary Grays
Photo: Courtesy of Kerry McCashin Batty

Photo: Courtesy of Joan Hilsman

Pineapple Chutney Appetizer

Contributed by Joan Hilsman

INGREDIENTS | SERVES 12

1 whole pineapple
16 ounces cream cheese, softened
1 teaspoon curry powder
½ cup prepared chutney
½ teaspoon dried mustard
⅓ cup sliced almonds, toasted

DIRECTIONS

Cut pineapple in half, lengthwise, with leaves still attached. Scoop flesh out of half and chop into ½-inches pieces. Save remainder of pineapple for another use.

Add softened cream cheese, curry powder, chutney and mustard to chopped pineapple. Mix thoroughly.

Fill scooped out pineapple with mixture. Arrange toasted almonds on top. If desired, arrange almonds in overlapping rows to simulate outside of pineapple.

Can't beat the presentation of this one!

Soups & Salads

Photo: Courtesy of Moore County Historical Association Collection, Southern Pines, NC

Young's Road was named for an old farm and remains the home of big horse farms that train thoroughbreds for racing and other national and international equestrian events, including the Olympics. In this photo, circa 1920, the Moore County Hounds founders, Jim and Jack Boyd, and Katharine Boyd, Jim's wife, lead a foxhunt along the then unpaved Young's Road at Young's Farm. The Boyd brothers founded the hunt in 1914, after the death of their grandfather, James Boyd, a Pennsylvania coal merchant. The first James Boyd brought his wealthy family to Southern Pines at the turn of the century and purchased thousands of acres on the east side of the town. Boyd named his huge estate Weymouth Heights and Weymouth Woods. He and his descendants became civic leaders. He funded improvements to Midland Road that links Southern Pines to Pinehurst, while his daughter initiated a movement that resulted in a town library, garden club, and civic club.

Zuppa Matta

Contributed by Joan Hilsman

INGREDIENTS | SERVES 4

- 9 slices French bread
- ½ red onion, thinly sliced
- 2 ripe tomatoes (or 1 small can, 14.5 ounces)
- 1 cucumber, peeled and thinly sliced
- 4 radishes, sliced
- ¼ cup pitted Greek olives, halved
- 12 basil leaves, roughly torn
- 2 tablespoons red wine vinegar
- 6 tablespoons olive oil
- Salt and pepper to taste

DIRECTIONS

Soak bread in cold water for 10-15 minutes. Squeeze each slice to get rid of excess moisture.

Tear bread into small chunks. Place bread in bowl and add remaining ingredients. Toss.

Serve at room temperature.

From the old country.

Irina's Borscht

Contributed by Katie Walsh

INGREDIENTS

- 1 pound stew meat
- 2 tablespoons canola oil, divided
- 2 potatoes, cubed
- 4 cups beef broth
- 1 cup chopped onion
- 2 carrots, grated
- 1 large beet, grated
- 1 lemon, juiced
- 1 can (15.5 ounce) diced tomatoes, drained
- ¼ head green cabbage, chopped
- 1 tablespoon minced dill
- 2 cloves garlic, crushed

DIRECTIONS

Cut stew meat into 1-inch cubes. In large soup pot over medium-high heat, brown meat in 1 tablespoon oil. Lower heat to medium-low and cook until done. Add potatoes to meat and cover with beef broth. Bring to boil. Lower heat to simmer until potatoes are done.

Meanwhile, in medium pan over medium heat, add remaining oil and saute onions until translucent. Add carrots and beets, and stir. Add lemon juice, then crushed tomatoes. Simmer 10 minutes.

Add tomatoes, cabbage and dill to meat and potatoes (may substitute 2 teaspoons dried dill for fresh dill). Simmer until ready to serve. Just before serving, press two cloves garlic into soup and cover.

This is my daughter-in-law's delicious soup recipe. I make it often.

Photo: Courtesy of Jeanne Paine

Backstretch Beef Stock

Contributed by Kerry McCashin Batty

INGREDIENTS | YIELDS 2 quarts

- 3-5 pounds backstretch beef marrow bones
- 4 carrots, peeled and cut into 3-inch pieces
- 4 celery stalks, cut into 3-inch pieces
- 2 onions, halved and peeled
- 1 head garlic, halved
- 1 bunch flat leaf parsley (with stems and use a healthy fistful)
- 5-6 stems thyme (whole)
- 2 bay leaves
- Black pepper corns to taste (about a tablespoon preferred)

DIRECTIONS

Preheat oven to 450 F.

In 17-by-12-inch roasting pan, roast bones about 15 minutes, turning occasionally. Watch closely if using backstretch or other grass-fed beef as it cooks faster.

Add vegetables to pan around beef bones. Roast until vegetables are brown, about 25 minutes.

Transfer everything to large stockpot. Add cold water to cover. For added flavor, pour off and discard fat from roasting pan. Add about ½ cup water to pan and scrape up brown bits from bottom. Add to pot.

Bring to boil and simmer 4 hours. Occasionally skim fat and foam from top. Add water if vegetables are poking out of water (usually about 2 cups at some point). Strain. Use in 2 days or freeze for up to 3 months.

Can also add herbs and seasonings, just be sure to strain before using.

This recipe is great for freezing in different size containers for different needs – some large quart containers for soup, muffin molds hold about a cup which is great for rice, grains or when you need just a little bit.

We've had cows since the early 1980s and while we've been making burgers, steaks and stew for a long time, beef stock is a recent addition to our recipe box. What took us so long? After making this, we will never buy it from the store again. There is no comparison!

Photo: Courtesy of Landon Russell

Shawna Smith's Fresh Tomato Herb Soup

Contributed by Barb Schindler

INGREDIENTS | SERVES 6-8

2 tablespoons chives
1 onion, chopped
4 cloves garlic, minced
2-3 tablespoons olive oil
1 can (14.5 ounces) stewed tomatoes
2 large fresh tomatoes, skinned and cut
1 carrot, chopped
4 cups chicken broth
1 bay leaf
4-6 tablespoons minced parsley
1 tablespoon chopped basil
1 teaspoon thyme
½ teaspoon ground fennel
1 can (6 ounces) tomato paste
1 teaspoon orange zest
½ cup dry French bread crumbs (optional)
Salt and pepper to taste

DIRECTIONS

In large pan over medium-low heat, saute chives, onion and garlic in oil until tender. Add tomatoes, carrot, chicken broth and herbs. Simmer 30 minutes. Stir in tomato paste and orange zest.

Remove bay leaf, puree soup in blender, and return to pot. Add bread crumbs if desired. Salt and pepper to taste and garnish with additional chives.

I've made this soup often. It's very yummy after being outside in a cold barn – a winter comfort food.

Greek Lemon Soup

Contributed by Joan Hilsman

INGREDIENTS | SERVES 6

6 cups chicken or vegetable broth
½ cup uncooked white rice
3 egg yolks
¼ cup lemon or lime juice
Salt and pepper to taste

DIRECTIONS

In large pot over high heat, heat broth to boiling. Add rice and simmer 20-25 minutes. Do not overcook.

In bowl, mix egg yolks and lemon or lime juice. Add 2 cups hot broth. Whisk together and pour back into pot. Heat until steaming but not boiling. Remove from heat and season with salt and pepper. Serve hot or cold.

The easiest soup in the world. Very refreshing when served cold.

Photo: Courtesy of Joan Hilsman

Photo: Courtesy of Moore County Historical Association Collection, Southern Pines, NC

Ruth Hanna Strong's Squash and Sweet Potato Soup

Contributed by Marianne Price

INGREDIENTS | SERVES 12

2 sweet potatoes
1 winter squash (butternut, acorn or spaghetti)
2 cans (15 ounces each) lentils, white beans or other legume, rinsed and drained (or package of dried beans, soaked overnight)
1 tablespoon olive oil
1 large sweet onion, chopped
½ - ¾ pound Andouille sausage
Garlic to taste
¼ cup frozen green peas, minced
Balsamic vinegar to taste

DIRECTIONS

Preheat oven to 375 F.

Cut sweet potatoes and squash in half. Remove seeds from squash. Bake on 18-by-26-inch baking sheet for about 1 hour.

If using dried beans, cook until done. If using canned, rinse and drain beans.

In medium pan over medium-low heat, add olive oil and saute onion, sausage and garlic.

In blender, puree cooked potatoes, squash and beans, then place in large soup pot. Cook soup over medium-low heat until the right consistency and flavor, about 10-15 minutes.

Add peas on top just before serving. Don't reheat or overcook peas; this causes an awful color.

Drizzle balsamic vinegar over peas and soup as serving.

Ruth Strong is a friend from work. We've made her recipe many times.

Easy Slow Cooker Potato Soup

Contributed by Carmalee Scarpitti

INGREDIENTS | SERVES 6 hungry riders

3 cups canned chicken broth
2 pounds frozen hash brown potatoes
Salt and pepper to taste
3 cups milk
3 cups shredded cheddar cheese or Monterey Jack

DIRECTIONS

In slow cooker, combine chicken broth, potatoes, salt and pepper. Cook on high for 4 hours or until potatoes are soft.

Mash potatoes if desired. Add milk and cheese, and blend. Continue to cook until cheese melts.

This soup tastes great after a ride on a cold day!

Moma's Cream of Artichoke Soup

Contributed by Caroline Young

INGREDIENTS | SERVES 6-8

2 packages (9 ounces each) frozen artichokes
1 ½ cans (10.5 ounces each) mushroom soup
1 cup heavy cream
¼ cup chicken broth
¼ cup dry white wine

DIRECTIONS

Cook artichokes according to package instructions. Drain and chop. Combine with other ingredients. Chill.

Photo: Courtesy of Landon Russell

Reflections Farm Squash Soup

Contributed by Kriestin L. Kleinschmidt

INGREDIENTS | SERVES 4

1½ tablespoons butter
1 onion, chopped
1 stalk celery, chopped
1 carrot, chopped
2 potatoes, cubed
1 butternut squash, peeled, seeded and cubed
4 cups chicken stock
Salt and pepper to taste

DIRECTIONS

In large pot over medium heat, melt butter. Add onion, celery, carrot, potatoes and squash for 5 minutes, or until lightly browned. Pour chicken stock to cover vegetables. Bring to boil, then reduce heat to low. Cover pot and simmer 40 minutes.

In blender, puree soup. Return to pot, and mix in any remaining stock. Season with salt and pepper.

Add cheese of choice and croutons to soup as a top dressing.

Warm Your Heart Friendship Soup

Contributed by Cheryl Jasinski

INGREDIENTS | SERVES 4

½ pound bacon, fried and crumbled
1 small onion, sliced
1 cup processed American cheese, diced
¾ cup wild rice, cooked
1 can (10.5 ounces) cream of potato soup
1 can (10.5 ounces) cream of chicken soup
1 pint half-and-half
2 cups whole milk
Salt and pepper to taste

DIRECTIONS

Fry slices of onion. Melt cheese.

In large soup pot, add bacon, onion and cheese to rice, soups, half-and-half, milk, salt and pepper. Heat on medium-low while stirring.

Forty years ago I was boarding a flight in Miami to North Carolina. I was bringing a small plant to my mother when I dropped it in the girl's lap seated next to me. She burst into laughter – imagine that! The whole plane laughed. We became and still are best friends. She cooked this soup for my entire family that same winter. Great with hot bread before a chilly afternoon ride! Thank you, Chris.

Noel Lang (left) mingles with other hunters, including James Boyd (holding riding crop) in Southern Pines in the 1930s. The hunters are wearing the three different types of hats associated with fox hunting - bowler, top hat and hunting cap.

Taco Soup

Contributed by Marianne and Jeff Chulay

INGREDIENTS | SERVES 12

- 2 pounds ground beef or turkey (beef for more flavor)
- 1 package (1.25 ounces) dry taco seasoning mix
- 1 package (1.25 ounces) dry ranch salad dressing mix
- 2 cups water
- 1 large can (28 ounces) diced tomatoes
- 1 large can (28 ounces) diced tomatoes and green chilies
- 1 can (1.25 ounces) white hominy, undrained
- 2 cans (8 ounces each) ranch style beans, original, undrained

DIRECTIONS

In medium pan over medium heat, brown beef or turkey and drain off grease.

In large soup pot, combine meat, seasoning mixes and water. Cook 15-20 minutes.

Add tomatoes, hominy and beans. Bring to boil and simmer 10-15 minutes.

Serve in bowls with shredded cheese, avocados, sour cream, tortilla chips or chopped onions.

An easy soup to make for fox hunting breakfasts. It is like chili, only better.

Photo: Courtesy of Katie Walsh

Chilled Watermelon Soup
Contributed by Robin Savoie

INGREDIENTS | SERVES 6-8
4 cups watermelon, seeded and cubed
⅓ cup apple juice or peach cider
2 tablespoons lime juice
1 teaspoon fresh mint
2 tablespoons diced, fresh ginger
1 tablespoon honey (optional)
½ cup nonfat plain yogurt or sour cream

DIRECTIONS
In food processor, blend watermelon, juices, mint, ginger and honey until smooth, stopping to scrape down sides. Cover and chill 1 hour.

Serve in individual bowls with a dollop of yogurt or sour cream.

Cucumber Soup
Contributed by Nancy Chase Rogers

INGREDIENTS | SERVES 4-6
4 medium to large cucumbers
¼ cup sweet onion
1 can (10.5 ounces) pea soup (not split pea)
1 can (10.5 ounces) chicken bouillon
4 ounces sour cream
Salt and pepper
Fresh dill
Garlic salt (optional)

DIRECTIONS
Peel cucumbers. Slice and remove seeds. In blender, combine cucumbers, onion, pea soup, chicken bouillon and sour cream. Add salt and pepper to taste.

Once blended, top with fresh dill and a dash garlic salt.

Refrigerate before serving.

Photo: Courtesy of Moore County Historical Association Collection, Southern Pines, NC

Gazpacho Blanco
Contributed by Wendy Hopper

INGREDIENTS | SERVES 6-8
- 3 medium cucumbers, peeled, seeded and sliced
- 3 cups chicken broth, divided
- 3 cups sour cream (or half sour cream, half yogurt)
- 3 tablespoons white vinegar
- 1 clove garlic, minced
- Salt to taste

Garnish
- 2 tomatoes, peeled, seeded and chopped
- ¾ cup slivered almonds, toasted
- ½ cup sliced green onions, including tops
- ½ cup minced parsley

DIRECTIONS
In blender or food processor, combine cucumber and 1 cup chicken broth. Add remaining chicken stock, sour cream, vinegar and garlic and blend well. Chill. Add salt to taste after well chilled.

Serve in bowls with garnish on top.

This is so refreshing and delicious! A real keeper for summer entertaining, or just to have on a warm night.

Gazpacho
Contributed by Roger Nekton

INGREDIENTS
- 8 cups tomato juice
- 6 tablespoons salad oil
- 4 tablespoons wine vinegar
- 1 teaspoon salt
- ¼ teaspoon pepper
- 1 tablespoon Worcestershire sauce
- 1 large cucumber, chopped
- 1 medium sweet onion, finely chopped
- 1 large green pepper, chopped (to taste)
- 3 cloves garlic, minced
- 1 large tomato, chopped

DIRECTIONS
Combine all ingredients.

Refrigerate overnight.

Garnish with croutons, chopped pimiento and diced avocado if desired.

30 | MOORE COUNTY HORSE COUNTRY COOKING

Photo: Courtesy of Jeanne Paine

Shawna Smith's Chicken Salad

Contributed by Barb Schindler

INGREDIENTS | SERVES 6

2 boneless chicken breasts
½ onion, chopped
1 stalk celery
2 carrots
1 teaspoon sorrel
1 teaspoon sage
1 teaspoon chives
2 teaspoons basil
2 teaspoons oregano
Salt and pepper to taste
1 cup mayonnaise
3 tart apples (such as Granny Smith), cut into small pieces
3 cups red or green seedless grapes, cut in half
1 additional stalk celery, minced (optional)

DIRECTIONS

In large pot over medium heat, cook chicken breasts in water with onion, celery, carrot, sorrel, sage, chives, basil, oregano, salt and pepper for 15-20 minutes.

When done, cut chicken into cubes. Strain broth and refrigerate for another use.

Mix mayonnaise, salt and pepper. Combine with cubed chicken, apples, grapes and minced celery.

This simple chicken salad is a basic recipe for a summer lunch, prepped ahead and chilled, so after being outside on a summer day, I can come in, relax on the porch, and enjoy a cool treat. Can be eaten over lettuce as a salad, or slapped on some good French or sourdough bread for a tasty afternoon treat.

Photo: Courtesy of Janie Boland

Wisconsin Chicken, Cranberry and Wild Rice Salad

Contributed by Leslie and John Watschke

INGREDIENTS | SERVES 4-6

4 cups chicken broth
1 cup wild rice
1 bag (6 ounces) dried cranberries
2 cups chunked, cooked chicken
1 cup tiny frozen peas (or fresh peas, blanched)
Poppy seed salad dressing

DIRECTIONS

In large pot over medium heat, bring chicken broth to low boil. Add rice. Reduce heat, cover, and simmer about 45 minutes or until desired texture. Drain excess liquid. This should make about 3-4 cups cooked rice. Cool.

Add cranberries, chicken and peas to cooled rice. Drizzle and stir in prepared poppy seed dressing until all is lightly coated. Keep refrigerated until ready to serve.

I know, without a doubt, that our horses Martin and Charlie Brown greatly appreciate leaving the frozen Wisconsin tundra far behind and hauling down to Winter Hill Farm where they help us explore the endless beauty of The Walthour-Moss Foundation every winter. This is an easy salad or luncheon main dish that uses some of the best ingredients of Wisconsin. The only shoveling involved should be into your mouth with plenty of time for a ride or an afternoon nap in the grass and warm sun.

Photo: Courtesy of George Manley

Ann M. Boland's Tuna Fish Salad

Contributed by Janie Boland

INGREDIENTS | SERVES 4

1 can (12 ounces) white meat tuna
1 can (12 ounces) light tuna
1 small onion, chopped
2 stalks celery, chopped
1 teaspoon lemon juice (fresh is best)
Mayonnaise to taste

DIRECTIONS

Drain tuna and reserve juice for dog or cat. Combine tuna, onion, celery, lemon juice and mayonnaise.

Mix thoroughly, then refrigerate. Serve cold in sandwiches with lettuce.

There were rave reviews when my mother, Anne M. Boland, provided this for lunch at one of our early Carolinas Hound Shows at Mile Away. We had moved from Hoffman to Southern Pines due to the generosity of Ginny Moss.

Moore County Hounds supporters provided lunch for Hound Show exhibitors. I served as Secretary and then co-Chairman for 14 years. People asked me about the tuna fish salad and the recipe. Mom said I could give it out. You can make it in various quantities. This is the base. The key is two kinds of tuna.

Photo: Courtesy of Moore County Historical Association Collection, Southern Pines, NC

Cucumber Sour Cream Salad

Contributed by Cameron Sadler

INGREDIENTS | SERVES 4

2 cucumbers, thinly sliced
½ cup sour cream
2 tablespoons lemon juice
½ teaspoon salt
½ teaspoon sugar
Pinch cayenne
Grated onion to taste

DIRECTIONS

Combine ingredients and chill.

Finnish Beet Salad

Contributed by Roger Nekton

INGREDIENTS | SERVES 4

1 cup cooked, diced beets
2 cups cooked, diced potato
¾ cup cooked, diced carrots
¼ cup chopped herring or anchovies
¼ cup champagne vinegar
Salt and pepper to taste
Lettuce
1 egg, hard cooked, chopped (or more to taste)

DIRECTIONS

Combine all ingredients except lettuce and egg. Chill 4 hours.

Serve in lettuce cup with egg sprinkled on top.

Irene Greenberg's Strawberry Spinach Salad

Contributed by Amy Bresky

INGREDIENTS | SERVES 6-8

- 2 tablespoons sesame seeds
- 1 tablespoon poppy seeds
- ½ cup sugar
- ½ cup olive oil
- ¼ cup white wine vinegar
- ¼ teaspoon paprika
- ¼ teaspoon Worcestershire sauce
- 1 tablespoon onion, minced
- 1 bag (10 ounce) spinach, chopped
- 1 quart strawberries, sliced
- ¼ cup toasted almonds

DIRECTIONS

In jar, add sesame seeds, poppy seeds, sugar, olive oil, vinegar, paprika, Worcestershire sauce and onion. Shake to mix, then refrigerate until chilled.

In large bowl, combine spinach, strawberries and almonds. Pour dressing over salad, toss, and refrigerate 10-15 minutes before serving.

Marinated Kale Salad with Gouda and Apples

Contributed by Robin Savoie

INGREDIENTS

- ¼ cup lemon juice
- ¼ cup olive oil
- 2 teaspoons honey
- ¼ teaspoon kosher salt
- ¼ teaspoon freshly ground pepper
- 2 Pink Lady or Gala apples
- 2 bunches (8 ounces) kale, stemmed and chopped
- ¼ cup aged Gouda cheese, shaved

DIRECTIONS

Whisk together lemon juice, olive oil, honey, salt and pepper.

Core apples, slice into rings, and cut into bite-sized pieces. Combine chopped kale and apples with dressing. Toss well.

Cover and chill 2 to 24 hours.

Add cheese and toss just before serving.

Baba's Cranberry Salad

Contributed by Jackie Rimmler

INGREDIENTS

- 2 packages (3 ounces each) raspberry flavored gelatin (feel free to substitute favorite flavors or mix)
- 1 can (14 ounces) whole cranberry sauce
- 1 can (11 ounces) mandarin oranges, drained
- 1 cup pecans (or substitute nut)

DIRECTIONS

Make gelatin according to package directions. Use bowl or mold about twice as large as needed to make gelatin.

Allow to set in refrigerator for 1½ hours or until getting firm. Stir cranberry sauce to break it up. Gently stir in cranberry sauce, oranges and pecans. Let set completely before serving.

Recipes from my dad are a favorite in our house. This recipe is simple, and making it brings back fond memories of him, especially on holidays when we are thankful for so much – including our horses and the WMF!

Fruit Salad

Contributed by Sandra C. Phillips

INGREDIENTS | SERVES 6-8

- 3 Honey Crisp apples, peeled, cored, and cut into one-inch cubes
- 3 ripe mangos, peeled, cored, and cut into one-inch cubes
- 1 large lime, juiced
- 1 tablespoon grated ginger
- Fresh mint leaves, chopped (amount to taste)
- 3-4 tablespoons raw honey

DIRECTIONS

In bowl, mix cubed apples and mangos with lime juice, ginger, mint and honey.

Salad is delicious with pork tenderloin or for brunch with sausage-egg-brie casserole. Can also be served over mesclun greens.

Friends who are gluten-free will enjoy this!

Photo: Courtesy of Claudia Coleman

Zippy Corn Salad
Contributed by Claudia Coleman

INGREDIENTS
- 1 pound chorizo or kielbasa sausage, cooked
- 1 pound frozen or canned corn
- 1 pound chickpeas, frozen or canned
- 1 red and green sweet pepper, chopped
- 2 stalks celery, chopped
- 1 onion, chopped
- 1 bunch cilantro, chopped
- Olive oil and balsamic vinegar dressing
- ¼ teaspoon cumin

DIRECTIONS
Slice sausage into ¼-inch pieces. Quickly cook frozen corn and chickpeas. If using canned, just drain and rinse.

Heat dressing. Add cumin. Pour into salad and mix well.

Chill and serve.

Mom's Crab Salad
Contributed by Cameron Sadler

INGREDIENTS | SERVES 4
- 1 pound crabmeat
- Mayonnaise
- 1 cup celery, chopped
- ½ cup onion, chopped
- 1 tablespoon dill
- 1 tablespoons lemon juice
- 2 tablespoons Worchestershire sauce
- Salt and pepper to taste

DIRECTIONS
In bowl, mix ingredients to taste.

Mom's Pasta Salad

Contributed by Roger Nekton

INGREDIENTS

- 2 pounds bowtie pasta, cooked
- 1 cup chopped celery
- 2 green peppers, chopped
- 2 cucumbers, chopped
- 1 medium onion, diced
- 2 tomatoes, chopped
- 2 large carrots, diced
- 2 cups peas, slightly cooked
- 1 can (15 ounces) mandarin orange slices, drained
- 4 cups chicken, cooked and chopped

Dressing
- 2 tablespoons mayonnaise or sour cream
- 1-3 teaspoons balsamic vinegar
- 1 tablespoon mustard
- 2 teaspoons sugar
- Salt and pepper to taste

DIRECTIONS

In large bowl, combine ingredients. In separate bowl, combine dressing ingredients, mixing well. Add to pasta salad. Let cool and serve.

My mom didn't use amounts, so adjust accordingly for number of people.

Tuna Macaroni Salad

Contributed by Mickey Wirtz

INGREDIENTS | SERVES 4

- 1 cup elbow macaroni, uncooked
- ¼ cup bottled French dressing
- 1 can or package (12 ounces) tuna, drained
- ½ cup diced green pepper
- ½ cup diced cucumber
- ¼ cup sliced radishes
- 1 teaspoon onion salt
- ⅛ teaspoon pepper
- 2 tablespoons lemon juice
- ¼ cup sour cream
- Salad greens

DIRECTIONS

Cook macaroni following package instructions. Drain well. In large bowl, toss with French dressing. Refrigerate, covered, 2-3 hours.

Add tuna, green pepper, cucumber, radishes, onion salt, pepper, lemon juice and sour cream to chilled macaroni. Toss to combine well.

Refrigerate until well chilled, at least 1 hour. Serve garnished with salad greens.

Caesar Salad

Contributed by Tricia Greenleaf

INGREDIENTS

1 French baguette (13 ounces)
1 stick (8 tablespoons) butter
1 tablespoon garlic paste
1 egg
¾ cup olive oil
1 tablespoon Worcestershire sauce
1 teaspoon spicy mustard
5 cloves garlic, pressed
Juice of 1 lemon
5 anchovies
Salad greens
1 cup grated Parmesan cheese

DIRECTIONS

For croutons, slice baguette and dry until stale. In medium pan over high heat, saute dried bread slices in garlic and butter. Set aside.

For dressing, whisk egg, olive oil, Worcestershire sauce, mustard, garlic, lemon juice and anchovies in bowl. Pour over salad greens. Top with Parmesan cheese.

This is my girlfriend's (and my) favorite Caesar salad recipe. It is yummy. I've been making it for 26 years and it's still on the same yellow paper she wrote it on ... I can't seem to part with it!

Vermicelli Vinaigrette

Contributed by Suzanne Powell

INGREDIENTS

8 ounces vermicelli spaghetti, broken in half
½ cup extra-virgin olive oil
¼ cup red wine vinegar
1 large clove garlic, minced
¼ teaspoon salt
⅛ teaspoon pepper
¼ teaspoon dried basil, crushed
1 jar (6 ounces) marinated artichoke hearts, drained and chopped
1 cup fresh mushrooms, sliced
2 tomatoes, peeled and cut up
½ cup chopped walnuts, toasted
2 tablespoons snipped parsley

DIRECTIONS

Cook pasta as package directs. Rinse and drain.

In jar, combine oil, vinegar, garlic, salt, pepper and basil. Shake well. Toss ⅓-cup of dressing with pasta. Cover and chill. Toss remaining dressing with artichokes and mushrooms. Cover and chill.

To serve, toss together pasta, artichoke mix, tomatoes, walnuts and parsley.

Serve in a lettuce-lined bowl.

Photo: Courtesy of Moore County Historical Association Collection, Southern Pines, NC

Sides

Corn Pudding

Contributed by Marianne Price

INGREDIENTS

2 tablespoons butter
1 ½ tablespoons flour
1 cup milk
2 cups canned corn, drained
1 tablespoon sugar
1 teaspoon salt
⅛ teaspoon pepper
2 eggs, well beaten

DIRECTIONS

Preheat oven to 350 F.

In medium pan, melt butter over medium-high heat. Add flour, and mix well.

Add milk gradually and bring to boiling point, stirring constantly. Let thicken.

Add corn, sugar, salt and pepper.

Heat thoroughly, then remove from heat.

Add eggs and pour into greased, 9-by-13-inch baking dish.

Bake covered until it bubbles, then uncover. Continue baking. Total baking time is 25 minutes, or until corn is firm.

Can be made a day ahead.

This recipe was my mother's (Marianne Bond) and probably my grandmother's (Fay MacAulay) before that. This one is always requested for Christmas dinner. I double the recipe for holidays. When you double the recipe, plan to bake a bit longer.

Photo: Courtesy of Katie Walsh

Tomato Pudding

Contributed by Tiffany Teeter

INGREDIENTS | SERVES 2

3 slices stale bread
2 tablespoons butter
6 ounces tomato puree
4 tablespoons brown sugar
Pinch of salt

DIRECTIONS

Preheat oven to 375 F.

Break bread into small pieces and place in bottom of ungreased 9-by-9-inch baking dish with lid.

Melt butter and drizzle over bread crumbs.

In small saucepan over medium-low heat, combine tomato puree, sugar and salt. Bring to a simmer. Spoon over bread crumbs in dish. Cover and bake 20-25 minutes.

Do not lift lid.

Herbed Yogurt Baked Tomatoes

Contributed by Stephen Later

INGREDIENTS | SERVES 4

½ cup plain or vanilla nonfat yogurt
1½ teaspoons all-purpose flour
½ teaspoon dried whole marjoram
¼ teaspoon salt
¼ teaspoon ground pepper
2 large, unpeeled round red tomatoes
¼ cup grated Romano cheese

DIRECTIONS

Preheat oven to 400 F.

Combine yogurt, flour, marjoram, salt and pepper. Stir well and set aside. Core tomatoes and halve (cross-wise). Remove seeds with thumbs. Place tomato halves, cut side up, in an 8-by-8-inch baking dish coated with cooking spray.

Spoon 2 tablespoons of yogurt mixture into each half tomato. Sprinkle with cheese.

Bake 30 minutes or until lightly browned.

Hawfields Cranberry Chutney

Contributed by Mary Francis Tate

INGREDIENTS

- 4 cups (1 pound) fresh cranberries
- 1 cup water
- 2 ½ cups sugar
- 2 sticks cinnamon
- 6 whole cloves
- ½ teaspoon salt
- 1 cup golden raisins
- 2 tart green apples, thinly sliced
- 2 pears, thinly sliced
- ½ cup chopped celery
- ½ cup chopped walnuts
- 1 teaspoon grated lemon rind

DIRECTIONS

Wash and pick over cranberries. In large pot, place cranberries, water and sugar. Place cinnamon sticks and cloves in cheesecloth. Add to pot. Add salt. Bring to boil and cook 10 minutes until berries pop. Add raisins, apples, pears and celery. Continue to cook for 10-15 minutes, stirring occasionally.

Remove from heat. Add walnuts and lemon rind. Remove spices in cheesecloth.

Place in jars and seal.

Pictured is L.P. Tate
Photo: Courtesy of Kerry McCashin Batty

Grandmother's Pear Chutney

Contributed by Caroline Young

INGREDIENTS | YIELDS 12 pints

- ½ pound onion, sliced
- 4 pounds pears, cut up
- 2 pounds raisins
- ½ teaspoon ground mace
- ½ teaspoon ground cinnamon
- ½ teaspoon ground cloves
- 1 ½ teaspoons ginger
- 1 ½ teaspoons paprika
- 1 ¼ teaspoons cayenne
- 2 ounces chopped garlic
- 2 ounces salt
- 3 ¼ pounds sugar

DIRECTIONS

In large saucepan, combine all ingredients. Simmer over medium heat for 3 hours.

Pour into jars and seal.

Photo: Courtesy of Caroline Young

Sweet Potato Soufflé

Contributed by Alice Cramer Glass

INGREDIENTS

3 cups sweet potatoes, cooked and mashed
1 cup sugar
1 cup crushed pineapple
½ cup evaporated milk
3 eggs
1 teaspoon vanilla
1 teaspoon salt
½ cup butter
1 teaspoon cinnamon
¼ teaspoon each ginger and nutmeg

Topping
1 cup brown sugar
1 cup chopped pecans
½ cup flour
½ cup butter

DIRECTIONS

Preheat oven to 400 F.

In mixing bowl, combine sweet potatoes, sugar, pineapple, milk, eggs, vanilla, salt, butter, cinnamon, ginger and nutmeg. Beat until smooth. Pour into buttered 2-quart soufflé dish.

Mix topping ingredients. Sprinkle over sweet potato mixture. Bake 10 minutes. Lower temperature to 350 F and cook an additional 45 minutes or until set in middle.

Sweet Potato Delight

Contributed by Wanda Little

INGREDIENTS

3 cups sweet potatoes, cooked and mashed
2 eggs
¼ cup butter, melted
1 cup sugar
½ cup milk
1 teaspoon salt

Topping
¼ cup butter
1 cup brown sugar
½ cup self-rising flour
1 cup chopped pecans

DIRECTIONS

Preheat oven to 350 F.

In bowl, mix potatoes, eggs, butter, sugar, milk and salt until well blended. Pour into buttered 9-by-13-inch baking dish.

For topping, melt butter and stir into brown sugar. Add flour and nuts, and mix until crumbly. Sprinkle on top of casserole. Bake 30 minutes.

Photo: Courtesy of Moore County Hounds

Kitty Walsh's Irish Potato Stuffing

Contributed by Chrissie Walsh Doubleday and Molly Walsh Robertson

INGREDIENTS
1 pound Idaho potatoes
1 package hot sausage
3 stalks celery, chopped
1 small onion, chopped
2 tablespoons poultry seasoning
Salt and pepper to taste

DIRECTIONS
Preheat oven to 350 F.

Peel and quarter potatoes. In large pan over high heat, boil potatoes until cooked, about 20-30 minutes. Drain and allow to dry in colander. Cover with dish towel to absorb excess moisture. Allow spuds to dry out before proceeding with the rest of the ingredients. Check after 30 minutes.

Once potatoes appear dry and flakey, place in large bowl, then add sausage little by little, mashing as you go along.

Add celery, onion and poultry seasoning, and mash into potato and sausage mixture.

Place stuffing into 9-by-13-inch baking dish and cook, covered, for 45 minutes. Uncover and cook an additional 15 minutes.

May also stuff turkey with some of stuffing and let it cook with the turkey.

Youngs Road Scalloped Cheese Potatoes

Contributed by Pam Jensen

INGREDIENTS

- 4 cups peeled and thinly sliced Yukon Gold potatoes
- 1 stick butter, cubed
- 4 tablespoons flour
- 2 teaspoons salt
- 3 teaspoons freshly ground black pepper
- 2 cups half-and-half, cream or milk
- 4 cups grated cheddar cheese, divided
- Pinch nutmeg

DIRECTIONS

Preheat oven to 375 F.

In well-greased, 9-by-9-inch baking pan, layer bottom with potatoes.

Mix 3 cups cheese with butter, flour, salt, pepper and half-and-half. Evenly layer remaining ingredients with potatoes.

Cover with foil. Bake 35-40 minutes or until potatoes are fork tender and sauce is thickened. Increase oven temperature to 400 F.

Remove cover and sprinkle top of potatoes with remaining cheese. Return to oven and bake until cheese is golden brown.

Garnish with chopped chives or parsley.

Mrs. Martin's Curried Shrimp in Avocado Halves

Contributed by Caroline Young

INGREDIENTS | SERVES 4

- 1-2 avocados
- 1 tablespoon lime juice, to taste
- 1 tablespoon butter
- 1 teaspoon curry powder
- 1 teaspoon salt
- ⅓ cup chopped onion
- 1 large tomato, chopped
- 1 pound shrimp, peeled and deveined
- 1 cup sour cream
- 2 cups rice, cooked

DIRECTIONS

Preheat oven to 300 F.

Brush avocado halves (or quarters) with lime juice. Place in shallow, 9-by-9-inch baking pan. Bake 10 minutes.

In small saucepan, combine butter, curry powder, salt, onion and tomato. Cook until onion is tender. Add shrimp and heat. Blend in sour cream. Place avocado on top of bed of warm rice. Fill avocado halves with curried shrimp.

Mrs. T. L. Martin was Moma's great friend.

Holiday Asparagus
Contributed by Mary Strasser

INGREDIENTS | SERVES 6-8

- 2 packages (8 ounces each) frozen asparagus
- 1 can (10.25 ounces) cream of mushroom soup
- 2 tablespoons milk
- 1 teaspoon Worcestershire sauce
- ¼ teaspoon salt
- ⅛ teaspoon pepper
- 1 can (8 ounces) water chestnuts, drained
- 1 can (4 ounces) sliced mushrooms, drained
- 1 jar (2 ounces) diced pimientos, drained
- 1 can (2.8 ounces) fried onion rings

DIRECTIONS

Thaw and drain asparagus, then cut into quarters. Set aside.

To create sauce, combine soup, milk, Worcestershire sauce, salt and pepper. Mix well and set aside.

In greased 8–by-8-inch baking dish, layer half of asparagus, water chestnuts, mushrooms, pimiento and sauce. Repeat layers. Cover and refrigerate. Remove from refrigerator and let stand for 30 minutes.

Preheat oven to 350 F.

Sprinkle dish with onion rings. Bake uncovered for 25 minutes.

Asparagus Parmesan
Contributed by Carol Butler

INGREDIENTS | SERVES 6-8

- 2 green onions
- ¼ cup butter
- 1 tablespoon flour
- ½ teaspoon salt
- Dash pepper
- 2 cans (15 ounces each) asparagus spears, drained, reserve juice
- ½ cup light cream
- 2 tablespoons diced pimiento
- ½ cup grated Parmesan cheese

DIRECTIONS

Preheat oven to 400 F.

In medium pan, saute onions in butter over medium-low heat. Stir in flour, salt and pepper. Add ½ cup asparagus juice and cream. Cook until thick. Add pimiento.

Arrange drained asparagus in 9-by-13-inch baking dish. Pour sauce over asparagus and top with Parmesan cheese.

Bake 20 minutes.

Mandy's Mayo

Contributed by Mandy Misner

INGREDIENTS

- 1 extra large farm fresh egg or 2 small bantam eggs
- ½ teaspoon Worcestershire sauce
- ¾ teaspoon sea salt or to taste
- Juice from 1 organic lemon
- ¾ cup extra-virgin olive oil *
- 1 cup sunflower seed oil
- 1 teaspoon vinegar of your choice (cider, red wine, balsamic or champagne)
- 1 tablespoon mustard of your choice (whole grain, Dijon or yellow)

DIRECTIONS

Beginning with the egg(s), place all ingredients in a wide mouth jar or blender cup. Using a stick blender, start at the bottom layer of egg, turn on the blender, and run up and down 2 times. Firmness will depend on how long its blended.

I like it creamy so I usually finish combining the last little bit of oil with a spoon. May store in the jar.

* I use the olive oil for perceived health reasons. The mayo has a slight olive oil flavor. You could use all sunflower seed oil for a more neutral flavor. I have substituted bacon fat for part of the oil or coconut oil. I recommend pastured pork bacon fat with no nitrates added.

Add to your mayo to taste. Some that I've tried include red and black pepper, lemon zest, chopped garlic, fish sauce, parsley, cilantro, thyme, chipotle chili peppers, wasabi powder, lime zest or lime juice.

I haven't purchased mayo in more than 10 years because it's so easy to make and delish. This mayo does contain raw eggs from my chickens. My family, including my 90-something mother-in-law, chooses to eat it over store bought mayo. Keeps up to a week.

Spinach and Artichoke Casserole

Contributed by Chuck Grubb

INGREDIENTS

2 packages (9 ounces each) frozen chopped spinach
½ cup butter, melted
1 package (8 ounces) cream cheese, softened
1 teaspoon lemon juice
1 can artichokes, drained (either bottoms or hearts)
Cracker crumbs
Butter

DIRECTIONS

Cook spinach by package directions. Drain well and place in bowl.

Add butter, cream cheese and lemon juice to spinach and blend together.

Place artichokes in bottom of greased 9-by-13-inch baking dish. Add spinach mixture. Top with cracker crumbs and dot with butter. Bake 25 minutes.

Recipe can easily be doubled.

"Try with all of your might – work very, very hard – to make the world a better place. And if your efforts are to no avail – no hard feelings!"

— HH The Dalai Lama

Aretha Fuller's Squash Casserole

Contributed by Caroline Young

INGREDIENTS | SERVES 4

1 pint cooked squash, mashed
1 small onion
3 tablespoons butter
2 eggs, beaten
½ cup grated cheese
Seasoned salt to taste
Pepper to taste
½ cup biscuit crumbs, sauteed in butter

DIRECTIONS

Preheat oven to 325 F.

In bowl, combine squash, onion, butter, eggs and cheese. Season with salt and pepper, and cover with sautéed crumbs in 1-quart baking dish.

Cook uncovered for 30 minutes or until bubbly.

Aretha lived at Pawleys Island and worked for the Halters.

Photo: Courtesy of Moore County Historical Association Collection, Southern Pines, NC

Spaghetti-less Spaghetti

Contributed by Mrs. Anne Devon Burnore

INGREDIENTS | SERVES 6-8

1 large spaghetti squash
2 strips raw bacon
1 pound ground turkey or chicken
2 tablespoons olive oil
1 cup chopped onions
½ package mushrooms, sliced
1 cup chopped bell peppers (green, red and yellow)
1 teaspoon crushed red pepper
1 tablespoon oregano (or ¼ cup freshly chopped)
1 teaspoon basil
2 teaspoons crushed garlic (or 4 finely minced cloves)
2 cups diced tomatoes, canned or fresh, seeded
Salt and pepper to taste
Parmesan cheese for topping

DIRECTIONS

Pierce spaghetti squash multiple times, ensuring punctures go deep enough to vent steam. Microwave 10-12 minutes, or until squash gives to the touch. Alternatively, bake at 350 F for 30-45 minutes, or until squash is soft.

Split spaghetti squash lengthwise. Scoop out strings and seeds. Using a fork, gently scrape inside of squash to create spaghetti-like strands. Scoop out strands and place in large bowl. Set aside.

Place bacon in large skillet and heat on high until pan is greased. Add ground turkey or chicken, and heat on medium-high until cooked thoroughly. Discard bacon appropriately (feed to hounds).

In medium skillet over high heat, sauté olive oil for 2 minutes. Add onions, mushrooms, peppers, red pepper, oregano, basil and garlic. Simmer until onions are light brown and mushrooms soften and darken. Lower heat to medium and add tomatoes. Simmer 5 minutes, stirring occasionally.

Combine meat and tomato sauce. Pour sauce over the spaghetti-less spaghetti and toss together. Serve as you would spaghetti with Parmesan as garnish.

Photo: Courtesy of Jeanne Paine

California Rice Casserole

Contributed by Danielle Veasy

INGREDIENTS | SERVES 6-8

- 1 cup chopped onion
- ¼ cup (½ stick) butter
- 4 cups cooked rice, cooled
- 1 cup sour cream
- 1 cup cottage cheese
- ½ teaspoon salt
- ⅛ teaspoon pepper
- 1 can (4 ounces) chopped green chilies
- 1 can (4 ounces) chopped black olives
- 2 cups shredded cheddar cheese

DIRECTIONS

Preheat oven to 375 F.

In large pan over medium-low heat, sauté onion with butter for 5 minutes. Remove from heat. Stir in cooked rice, sour cream, cottage cheese, salt, pepper, green chilies and olives.

Put half of rice mixture in buttered 9-by-13-inch baking dish. Top with 1 cup cheese. Repeat.

Bake uncovered 25-30 minutes.

Grittman Family Rice Consommé

Contributed by Brooke Maiello

INGREDIENTS

- 1 cup rice
- 2 cans beef consommé
- 1 large can (13.25 ounces) mushrooms stems and pieces
- 1 medium onion, chopped
- ¾ stick (6 tablespoons) butter, sliced

DIRECTIONS

Preheat oven to 350 F.

Pour rice into 9-by-9-inch baking dish. Add consommé. Add drained mushrooms and chopped onion.

Top with sliced butter. Let stand about 15 minutes.

Bake 45 minutes.

Great with grilled chicken and green beans.

Baked Vidalia Onions

Contributed by Anne Webb

INGREDIENTS | SERVES 1

1 Vidalia onion
Sprinkle of soy sauce
1 tablespoon butter
Pinch sugar

DIRECTIONS

Preheat oven to 350 F.

Cut off top and bottom of onion. Peel, then cut through in quarters, almost to the bottom.

Sprinkle with soy sauce. Add butter and sugar.

Wrap onion in foil and bake 35-40 minutes.

Red Onion Salad

Contributed by Anne Webb

INGREDIENTS | SERVES 12

6-7 large onions, sliced (4 cups)
Margarine for sauteeing
½ cup ketchup
¼ cup vegetable oil
¼ cup cider vinegar
2-3 tablespoons sugar

DIRECTIONS

In medium pan over medium-low heat, saute onions 5-10 minutes in margarine until limp, but do not brown. Drain on paper towels and place in bowl.

Cover with ketchup, oil, vinegar and sugar.

Place in refrigerator for 2 hours or longer.

Moore County Potato Salad

Contributed by Helen Kalevas

INGREDIENTS | SERVES 10

- 10 medium-sized red potatoes
- ¾ cup mayonnaise
- 6 dill pickles, chopped
- 2 tablespoons pickle juice (or more to taste)
- 1 tablespoon good quality yellow mustard
- 1 dash of celery salt or seed
- 1 generous teaspoon fresh, chopped dill
- Salt and pepper to taste
- 5 hard boiled eggs, chopped small
- Green onions and parsley for garnish (optional)

DIRECTIONS

In saucepan, place whole potatoes and cover with an inch of water. Boil potatoes about 20-25 minutes until cooked through and firm, but not crisp (overcooking will break skin). Allow to cool completely. Once cool, chop, skin on, into bite-sized pieces. Place in serving bowl.

Add mayonnaise, pickles, pickle juice, mustard, celery salt or seed, dill, salt and pepper. Blend thoroughly with a large spoon. Add eggs and mix gently so as not to break up egg pieces.

I recommend making it a day ahead or allowing it to chill several hours before serving. Stir occasionally to blend flavors. Jazz this recipe up by using Peruvian blue or purple potatoes.

Since I moved to Southern Pines in 2009 to hunt with Moore County Hounds, this was my signature dish for summer potlucks, tailgates and Kentucky Derby parties. One friend liked it so much that I made it for her for Christmas every year. Hellmann's® Mayonnaise and pickle juice are the keys to this recipe.

Kickin' Cucumber Salad

Contributed by Brooke Maiello

INGREDIENTS

- 1 jalapeno pepper, seeded
- 2 cloves garlic, finely minced
- 4 tablespoons minced cilantro
- 3 tablespoons fresh lime juice
- 3 cucumbers, peeled and thinly sliced
- ¼ teaspoon crushed red pepper
- ½ teaspoon salt (or to taste)
- Pepper to taste
- 3 tablespoons olive oil

DIRECTIONS

Finely dice jalapeno. In bowl, combine jalapeno, garlic, cilantro and lime juice.

Slice cucumbers and add to bowl. Stir to combine. Serve immediately or let marinate in refrigerator for a couple of hours

We love to use cucumbers, jalapenos and cilantro from our garden. This is one of my favorite sides to have in my cooler at local horse shows. It goes well with just about anything. We love it with our slow cooker chicken on a roll for a snack between classes.

54 | MOORE COUNTY HORSE COUNTRY COOKING

Photo: Courtesy of Moore County Historical Association Collection, Southern Pines, NC

Pictured are Fred McCashin, John McCashin and Jimmy Hatcher. John and Jimmy Judges for 1st NCVRF Horse Show Photo: Courtesy of Kerry McCashin Batty

Curried Fruit Bake

Contributed by Mary Strasser

INGREDIENTS | SERVES 12

- 1 large can (29 ounces) pear halves
- 2 large cans (29 ounces each) peach halves
- 1 large can (20 ounces) pineapple slices
- 6 maraschino cherries
- ½ cup melted butter
- 1 cup light brown sugar
- 2 teaspoons curry powder

DIRECTIONS

Preheat oven to 300 F.

Pour off juices and drain fruit on paper towels. Dry well. Arrange alternating pears and peaches with pit side down in an 11-by-7-inch baking dish.

Place pineapple rings on top with cherries in the holes. Mix together butter, brown sugar and curry powder, and spread over fruit.

Bake uncovered 1 hour. Refrigerate overnight.

Next day, reheat at 325 F for 30 minutes. Serve hot in baking dish with pork chops or chicken.

Delicious Macaroni and Cheese

Contributed by Elizabeth Rose

INGREDIENTS | SERVES 6-8

- 2 cups cooked macaroni
- 2 ½ - 3 cups grated cheddar cheese
- 4 tablespoons melted butter
- Salt and pepper to taste
- 2 ½ cups milk
- 2 eggs

DIRECTIONS

Preheat oven to 350 F. Grease 2 ½-quart baking dish.

In bowl, mix macaroni, cheese, melted butter, salt and pepper.

In separate bowl, mix milk and eggs.

Combine and place in baking dish.

Cover top with extra cheese and bake 45-60 minutes.

Photo: Courtesy of Elizabeth Rose

Mac and Cheese ... the Best Ever!

Contributed by Jane Simon

INGREDIENTS

6 slices white bread
8 tablespoons unsalted butter, divided
1 pound elbow macaroni
½ cup flour
3 ½ cups milk
4 ½ cups (18 ounces) grated sharp white cheddar cheese, divided
2 cups (8 ounces) grated Gruyere cheese, divided
2 teaspoons salt
¼ teaspoon nutmeg
¼ teaspoon pepper, freshly ground
¼ teaspoon cayenne pepper (can substitute paprika)

DIRECTIONS

Preheat oven to 375 F. Butter a 3-quart baking dish.

Remove crust from bread. Tear into large pieces and pulse a few times in processor to form large crumbs. Transfer to large bowl. Add 2 tablespoons melted butter. Toss to coat. Set aside.

Cook macaroni for 5 minutes. Drain and run under cold water.

In medium sauce pan over medium heat, heat milk.

Melt 6 tablespoons butter in skillet. When it bubbles, add flour. Cook and stir 1 minute. Do not let flour darken. Heat milk. While whisking butter and flour mixture, pour in hot milk.

Cook and continue whisking until mixture becomes thick, 2 to 3 minutes. Remove from heat. Whisk in 3 cups cheddar and 1 ½ cups Gruyere cheese. Add salt, nutmeg, pepper, and cayenne pepper or paprika.

Stir macaroni into cheese sauce. Pour in baking dish. Sprinkle with remaining cheese and top with bread crumbs.

Bake 30 minutes.

Wonderful to make in the morning and bake later after trail riding. You will need to add extra bake time if it is cold.

Mrs. Ellison McKissick Jr.'s Broccoli Soufflé

Contributed by Caroline Young

INGREDIENTS | SERVES 6

¼ cup butter
¼ cup sifted flour
1 ¼ cups milk
½ cup grated American cheese
5 eggs, separated
1 ½ teaspoons salt
⅛ teaspoon minced garlic
1 ½ cups chopped cooked broccoli
2 tablespoons lemon juice

DIRECTIONS

Preheat oven to 350 F.

In medium saucepan over low heat, make a cream sauce with butter, flour and milk. Add cheese. Remove from heat. Add egg yolks, well beaten with ½ teaspoon salt. Add garlic, broccoli and lemon juice.

Sprinkle egg whites with 1 teaspoon salt and beat until stiff. Fold in cheese mixture and mix until blended.

Bake 1 hour in well-greased 1 ½-quart baking dish that has been placed in 1 inch of hot water.

This is Moma's recipe.

Cowboy Beans

Contributed by Jane Simon

INGREDIENTS | SERVES 6-8

- 1 pound ground beef
- 1 onion, chopped
- ½ cup ketchup
- ½ cup brown sugar
- 1 teaspoon vinegar
- 1 tablespoon molasses
- ½ cup water
- 1 teaspoon dry mustard
- 1 can (15 ounces) pork and beans
- 1 can (15 ounces) baby lima beans
- 1 can (15 ounces) kidney beans
- ½ pound bacon, cooked and crumbled

DIRECTIONS

Preheat oven to 300 F.

Brown ground beef with onion and drain.

In bowl, mix ketchup, brown sugar, vinegar, molasses, water and dry mustard, then add to cooked beef mixture. Mix next six ingredients together and add to cooked beef mixture.

Partially drain beans and add to beef mixture. Add bacon.

Stir together all ingredients and place in a 4-quart baking dish. Cook 2 to 3 hours in oven.

I usually double or triple this for large gatherings after riding.

Sausage Stuffed Mushroom Caps

Contributed by Janie Carroll

INGREDIENTS

- 2 pounds portabella mushrooms
- 1 pound bulk sausage
- 8 ounces cream cheese, room temperature
- ½ cup shredded cheese (Swiss, cheddar or flavor of choice)

DIRECTIONS

Preheat oven to 350 F.

Rinse and dry mushrooms. Remove stems from caps. Place caps in shallow roasting pan. Cut stems into small pieces.

Brown sausage, add stems, and saute until tender. Drain grease from sausage.

Add cheeses to sausage. Stuff each cap with desired amount. Bake 30 minutes.

Recipe can be halved; stuffing will keep refrigerated for a week.

Entrées

Photo: Courtesy of Moore County Historical Association Collection, Southern Pines, NC

Charlotte Wentworth Harvey's Canadian Goose

Contributed by Lynn Harvey

INGREDIENTS | SERVES 4-6

½ cup butter
1 cup diced carrots
1 cup diced celery
1 cup finely chopped onion
1 medium apple, cored, peeled and diced
4 cloves garlic, minced
1 cup chicken broth
½ cup Chardonnay
¼ cup chopped parsley
3 tablespoons poultry seasoning
2 tablespoons rosemary
2 tablespoons thyme
4 bay leaves
1 teaspoon salt
1 teaspoon black pepper
1 whole wild goose, about 6-10 pounds
8 potatoes, boiled

DIRECTIONS

Preheat oven to 375 F.

In large saucepan over medium low heat, melt butter. Add carrots, celery, onions, apple and garlic. Sauté 8-10 minutes. Add stock, wine, parsley, seasoning, rosemary, thyme, bay leaves, salt and pepper. Raise heat and bring to a boil, about 1 minute.

Reduce heat and simmer 6-8 minutes. Pour vegetables and liquid into a large roasting pan with cover. Turn bird breast side down into vegetables and liquid. Spoon some liquid and vegetables over goose and add more water (or wine if you like) to submerse bird halfway. Cover and roast about 75 minutes. Uncover and turn bird with breast up and cook an additional 15 minutes or until a meat thermometer registers 160 F when inserted beside leg bone in thigh.

Remove and let bird sit, about 10 minutes. Spoon broth and vegetables over each portion of sliced meat and boiled potatoes.

May also be served with favorite stuffing recipe cooked in separate dish.

Note: Wild goose is very lean and resembles beef, so it can't be cooked the same way as domestic goose, which is fatty.

Sand Chicken

Contributed by Pat Richardson

INGREDIENTS | SERVES 6

- 3 skinless, boneless chicken breasts, halved and trimmed to ½-inch thickness or less
- 1 cup flour
- Salt and pepper to taste
- 2 eggs, beaten
- 1 teaspoon minced garlic (or more to taste)
- 1 cup plain breadcrumbs
- 1 cup ground Parmesan cheese
- Caper for garnish

DIRECTIONS

Generously cover bottom of frying pan with butter and olive oil.

Trim and rinse breast pieces. Pat dry.

In bowl, combine flour, salt and pepper. In separate bowl, combine beaten eggs and garlic. In third bowl, combine breadcrumbs and Parmesan cheese.

One at a time, in order, roll breasts in flour mixture, dip in egg mixture and roll in breadcrumb mixture.

Let rest for 30 minutes.

In medium pan on low heat, fry chicken in olive oil and butter mixture. Do not cover. When breasts reach a golden color, check center. Serve with wedges of lemon and capers.

Our family calls it Sand Chicken, named by our daughter when she was 4, because it looks like it's covered in sand. What could be more appropriate to the Sandhills?

Catherine's Chicken Piccata

Contributed by Jean Rae Hinton

INGREDIENTS

- 1 cup flour
- 1 teaspoon salt
- ½ teaspoon paprika
- ¼ teaspoon pepper
- 1 package (4 breasts) thin cut chicken (scaloppini style)
- 3 tablespoons butter
- 3 tablespoons olive oil
- ½ cup white wine
- 3 tablespoons fresh lemon juice
- 3 tablespoons capers

DIRECTIONS

In zip-close bag, mix flour, salt, paprika and pepper.

Pound chicken and lightly toss in flour mixture.

In large skillet, melt butter and olive oil, being careful not to burn butter. Sauté pounded chicken on both sides in oil and butter until brown. Put in warming drawer or warm oven.

Add wine, lemon juice and capers to skillet and stir up bits. Reduce liquid. Pour over chicken. Serve or keep in low-temperature oven until time to serve.

Will hold for company or late husband. Once you make it the first time, this recipe becomes very easy.

Maggie Price's Chicken

Contributed by Marianne Price

INGREDIENTS | SERVES 6

1 can pitted black cherries
½ cup sherry
3 whole chicken breasts, halved
3 tablespoons olive oil
1 large or two small onions, diced
1 jar chili sauce
½ cup brown sugar
1–2 tablespoons Worcestershire sauce

DIRECTIONS

Preheat oven to 350 F.

Drain cherries. Soak in sherry.

In skillet, brown chicken breasts in olive oil. Place browned chicken in 9-by-13-inch baking dish.

Cover chicken with diced onions.

In bowl, mix chili sauce, brown sugar and Worcestershire sauce. Pour over chicken.

Bake, covered, 25-30 minutes.

Drain cherries. Place over top of chicken and continue to cook 10-15 minutes.

Option: You can cook in slow cooker at the lowest setting for 5-6 hours or up to 8 hours.

Maggie Price is my sister-in-law. She is a wonderful cook!

The Easiest Slow Cooker Chicken Ever

Contributed by Brooke Maiello

INGREDIENTS | SERVES 8

1 large onion, sliced
1 whole chicken

DIRECTIONS

Cover bottom of slow cooker with onion slices.

Place chicken on top of onion layer. Cook on low overnight or on high for 6 hours.

Carefully remove chicken and serve. May throw out onions.

As a young teen, a family friend insisted on my sidesaddle having a proper chicken sandwich in my box. This chicken is what she would set up the night before she went to show and hunt. In the morning, she would put it on white bread — plain of course! She made extras that went in the cooler for lunch to share. I make this at least once a week. I just start it in the morning, and dinner is done when I come in from the barn. Great with a cucumber salad!

Emeline Harvey's Sunday Chicken Dinner

Contributed by Lynn Harvey

INGREDIENTS | SERVES 6-8

1 tablespoon salt
1½ tablespoons poultry seasoning
1 whole free-range chicken
6 cups dry whole-wheat cubes
½ teaspoon salt
4 teaspoons poultry seasoning or to taste
1 small onion, chopped
1½ stalks celery, chopped
1 cup Chardonnay wine
1 cup water
1 bay leaf
6-7 whole carrots
1 large or 2 medium onions, cut into 6 wedges each
4-6 gold potatoes with skins

DIRECTIONS

Preheat oven to 350 F.

In bowl, mix bread, salt, poultry seasoning, onion and celery, and set aside. Place chicken in roasting pan. Rub seasoning onto bird and into both cavities. Stuff both cavities of bird mixture. Secure neck cavity with toothpicks. Tuck back and tie legs with cooking string. Add wine, water and bay leaf.

Cover roasting pan and place in oven for 3 hours. Baste three times at 45 minutes, 1 ½ hours, and 2 hours and 10 minutes. At 1½ hours, add carrots, onion wedges and potatoes.

Serve with gravy made from drippings.

Gravy

Drain liquid off bird into a frying pan. Leave heat off. Add 1/3 cup flour in a 1 cup liquid measure. Slowly add cold water to form a paste. Beat all lumps out with a spoon. Slowly add more cold water and continue beating until a pourable liquid thicker than gravy is formed. Make sure no lumps are visible.

Pour a little at a time into frying pan. Stir quickly to blend and to prevent lumps. When completely blended in, add more. Repeat until 1/2 inch of liquid are lumps are left in cup. Season gravy to taste.

Turn on heat and stir constantly until gravy thickens. If too thin, take off heat and make up more flour paste. Repeat process.

Javanese Rice Taffle (7 Boy Curry)

Contributed by Linda Dreher

INGREDIENTS | SERVES 12

8 cups coconut milk
4 cups flaked coconut
2 tablespoons butter
1 cup chopped onion
2 teaspoons ginger
2 cloves garlic, chopped
2 tablespoons curry powder
2 cups chicken stock
1 cup heavy cream
2 tablespoons rice flour
2 tablespoons cornstarch
Salt, pepper and paprika to taste
6 cups diced cooked chicken
3 cups sliced mushrooms
1 apple, peeled and chopped

DIRECTIONS

Scald coconut milk. Add flaked coconut. Let stand 2 hours.

In skillet, saute onions in melted butter. Add ginger, garlic and curry powder, and stir. Add coconut mixture, chicken stock and heavy cream.

In bowl, combine rice flour and cornstarch with a small amount of water. Stir until smooth. Add to onion mixture. Cook mixture to thicken. Add salt, pepper and paprika to taste.

Strain out coconut. Add diced, cooked chicken and mushrooms. Then add chopped apple.

Serve with Arborio rice and garnish with raisins, chopped peanuts, coconut, chopped boiled eggs, sliced green onions and chutney.

My mother, Betty Dreher, was a fabulous cook. The Javanese Taffle was one of her favorites that I feel honored to continue cooking, and always remember her in the process.

Turkey Meatloaf

Contributed by Susan Powell

INGREDIENTS | SERVES 6-8
- 3 tablespoons butter
- ½ large onion, diced
- 3 celery sticks, diced
- 1 tablespoon poultry seasoning
- Salt and pepper to taste
- 1 bag (12 ounces) stuffing mix
- ⅓ cup chicken stock
- 1 pound ground turkey
- 1 egg
- Olive oil

DIRECTIONS
Preheat oven to 375 F.

In large skillet over medium-low heat, sauté onions and celery in butter until translucent. Add poultry seasoning, salt and pepper. Add stuffing mix. Moisten with chicken stock. Allow to cool.

In large bowl, mix ground turkey, egg and stuffing mix. Form into loaf, place on baking sheet, and drizzle with olive oil.

Bake 1 hour.

This recipe goes back to my mother, not a fancy cook, but one of her best. With the weather this winter, comfort food was a go-to in our house, and this is one of my favorites. It's excellent served with turkey gravy.

Mimomma's Yummy Chicken

Contributed by Andrea Chisholm

INGREDIENTS | SERVES 8
- 8 chicken breast halves
- 1 can (16 ounces) whole cranberry sauce
- 1 packet (1.2 ounces) onion soup mix
- 8 ounces regular or fat-free French salad dressing

DIRECTIONS
Preheat oven to 350 F.

Place chicken in 9-by-13-inch baking dish prepared with cooking spray.

Combine cranberry sauce, soup mix and French dressing. Pour over chicken and bake, covered, for 1 hour. Cool slightly.

Refrigerate overnight. Reheat, covered, for 30 minutes.

Wild Duck with Orange Sauce

Contributed by Lynn Harvey

INGREDIENTS

1 wild duck, dressed and halved
1 cup broth or pan drippings
1 tablespoon cornstarch
1 cup freshly squeezed orange juice
2 tablespoons freshly squeezed lemon juice
Salt to taste

DIRECTIONS

Preheat oven to 300 F.

In roasting pan, brown duck with a small amount of fat by placing the side with the skin downward on rack inside roasting pan. Cover and roast for 1 ½ - 2 hours or until tender. Uncover during last 15 minutes to brown skin. Pour off broth, skim and discard fat. Set aside 1 cup of broth.

Make smooth, thin paste with cornstarch and cold water. Drizzle into broth in pan on top of stove. Add orange and lemon juice. Cook until thickened. Salt to taste. Pour over duck on a serving platter. Garnish with fresh orange slices.

Note: Domestic duck from the grocery store may be substituted.

Aunt Kitty's Doves

Contributed by Caroline Young

INGREDIENTS | SERVES 6-8

12 to 14 doves and giblets
Salt and pepper
Paprika
¼ cup flour
1 stick butter
½ cup dry sherry
Mushrooms (optional)

DIRECTIONS

In bowl, mix salt, pepper, paprika and flour, and dust doves. Melt butter in heavy pan. Brown doves on back side, then breast side.

Turn heat to low. Add giblets. Cover pan. May have to add water or a little more butter. Cook on low 2-3 hours.

Can stay on warm without harming them while guests move to the dinner table.

Five minutes before serving, add sherry. Also can add mushrooms to the gravy.

Photo: Courtesy of Moore County Historical Association Collection, Southern Pines, NC

Howe Family Holiday Oysters

Contributed by Susan Howe Wain

INGREDIENTS | SERVES 6

- ½ cup chopped onions
- 2 cups chopped celery
- 1 tablespoon chopped green pepper
- 3 tablespoons butter, plus 2 tablespoons
- 1 tablespoon flour
- ½ cup milk
- 3 cups wild rice, cooked
- ½ teaspoon thyme
- ¼ teaspoon sage
- ⅛ teaspoon pepper
- 1 pint oysters
- ½ cup breadcrumbs
- 1 cup cheese (optional)

DIRECTIONS

Blend breadcrumbs and 2 tablespoons butter. Set aside. In skillet, brown onions, celery and pepper in butter. Blend in flour. Add milk slowly. Stir in hot rice and seasonings.

Put in baking dish. Arrange oysters on top. Cover with buttered breadcrumbs. Broil until oysters curl. One cup cheese may be added to sauce if desired.

Stuffed Lobster

Contributed by Stephen Later

INGREDIENTS | SERVES 1

- 1½ pound lobster (per person)
- Butter, melted

Stuffing (per lobster)
- ⅔ cup breadcrumbs
- 2 shrimp, diced
- 2 tablespoons diced celery
- ¼ tablespoon seasoning salt

DIRECTIONS

Preheat oven broiler to 450 F.

In bowl, mix stuffing ingredients and set aside.

Clean lobster without breaking backs. Bake face down 12-15 minutes.

Remove from oven. Turn over (open middle with two forks) and stuff. Pour melted butter on stuffing and tail.

Broil lobsters an additional 12 minutes.

Baste meat and stuffing with butter.

15-Minute Whitefish

Contributed by Lynn Harvey

INGREDIENTS | SERVES 4

Celtic sea salt to taste (about ¼ teaspoon per fillet)
2 pieces (eight ounces each) haddock or halibut, or 4 (3-4 ounces each) tilapia fillets
1 teaspoon Old Bay shrimp boil seasoning (in the bag)
8 ounces Chardonnay

DIRECTIONS

Preheat oven to 400 F.

Salt fillets and place in 9-by-13-inch baking pan. Sprinkle Old Bay shrimp boil over fillets. Pour wine into pan, taking care not to wash off seasoning.

Cover with parchment paper and bake 15 minutes. Test fillets with fork for opaqueness in the center.

When opaque and white, fish is done. Serve with asparagus or your favorite vegetables.

Baked Fish

Contributed by Claire Rhodes

INGREDIENTS | SERVES 2-3

1 pound cod or haddock
2 tablespoons butter
1 package (4 ounces) butter crackers, crumbled
Salt and pepper to taste
Seasonings (optional)
1 tablespoon water

DIRECTIONS

Preheat oven to 450 F.

Melt butter in bottom of 11-by-7-inch pan. Roll fish in butter.

Coat fish on both sides with crushed cracker crumbs. Sprinkle with salt and pepper, and seasonings of choice.

Pour water in pan. Bake 10 minutes

Salmon with Honey Mustard Sauce

Contributed by Lynda Acker

INGREDIENTS

2 tablespoons minced shallots or green onions
1 tablespoon chopped fresh thyme, or 1 teaspoon dried
3 tablespoons honey
1 tablespoon spicy mustard
½ teaspoon salt
¼ teaspoon ground red pepper
4 6-ounce salmon fillets, about 1-inch thick
Thyme sprigs, if desired

DIRECTIONS

Prepare grill by coating rack with cooking spray and preheating on high.

In small bowl, combine shallots, thyme, honey, mustard, salt and red pepper. Brush mixture over skinless side of fish. Place fish on grill skin side up and grill 3 minutes. Flip fillets and lower heat to medium. Brush with sauce, and continue to grill for about 8 minutes or until cooked through.

Fish should flake easily with a fork. Garnish with thyme sprigs if desired.

I usually double or triple the amount of sauce to serve remainder at the table.

Spicy Shrimp Curry

Contributed by Monika Bargmann Brown

INGREDIENTS | SERVES 4-6

3 tablespoons olive oil
1 medium onion, thinly sliced
3 cloves garlic
1 can (14.5 ounces) fire-roasted canned tomatoes
⅓ can tomatoes with green chiles
14 ounces fresh tomatoes
1 teaspoon curry powder
2 teaspoon garam masala
1 pound fresh shrimp, peeled and deveined
1 pound white rice, cooked

DIRECTIONS

Heat oil in large, heavy, non-stick saucepan. Add onion and garlic for 10 minutes, until onions are translucent. Add tomatoes and spices. Cook, uncovered, on low heat 35-40 minutes, stirring occasionally.

Add shrimp and stir until shrimp are pink. Turn off heat and cover; allow to stand 5 minutes.

Serve over rice.

This recipe is from Natalie Cole of Royal Oak, Michigan.

Shrimp With Feta

Contributed by Mary Ellen Bailey

INGREDIENTS | SERVES 6

1 pound bowtie pasta
1 tablespoon olive oil
1 medium onion, diced
2 cloves garlic, minced
2 cans (14.5 ounces each) no-salt added diced tomatoes, with juice
¼ cup minced flat-leaf parsley
1¼ pounds medium shrimp, peeled and deveined
¼ teaspoon salt
¼ teaspoon freshly ground black pepper
1 cup crumbled feta cheese

DIRECTIONS

Preheat oven to 425 F.

Cook pasta. Drain and set aside.

In ovenproof skillet, heat oil over medium-high heat. Add onion and cook until softened, about 3 minutes. Add garlic and cook an additional minute. Add tomatoes and bring to a boil. Reduce heat to medium-low and let simmer, about 5 minutes, until tomato juice thickens.

Remove from heat. Stir in parsley, shrimp and pasta. Season with salt and pepper. Sprinkle feta over top. Bake until shrimp are cooked through and cheese melts, about 12 minutes.

This is a great dish for a large crowd. You can stretch it by adding more pasta, or more or less shrimp. I sauté my shrimp while the onion mixture is cooking, and then place the shrimp in last with the feta. I just put it in the oven long enough to melt the feta! Great with bread for dipping.

Cowpuncher Stew

Contributed by Andrea Moore

INGREDIENTS | SERVES 6

- 1½ pounds beef stew, cut in cubes
- 5 tablespoons flour, divided
- 2 teaspoons salt, divided
- 2 tablespoons shortening or oil
- 1½ tablespoons strong coffee (use instant coffee crystal after the first liquid measure to increase coffee taste if desired)
- 2 tablespoons molasses to taste
- 1 clove garlic, minced
- 1 teaspoon Worcestershire sauce to taste
- ½ teaspoon dried oregano
- ⅛ teaspoon cayenne pepper
- 1½ cups water, plus ¼ cup
- 4 carrots, sliced
- 4 small onions, quartered
- 3 medium potatoes, peeled & diced

DIRECTIONS

Coat beef with 2 tablespoons flour and 1 teaspoon salt. In skillet, brown in shortening or oil.

Add coffee, molasses, garlic, 1 teaspoon salt, Worcestershire sauce, oregano and cayenne.

Cover and simmer over low heat about 2 hours, or until beef is very tender.

Add 1½ cups water, carrots, onions and potatoes. Cover and simmer about 30 minutes until veggies are tender.

Blend ¼ cup water with 3 tablespoons flour. Add to stew to thicken.

Pictured are Libby Evans and Peter Doubleday
Photo: Courtesy of Kerry McCashin Batty

Cowboy Stew

Contributed by Janie Carroll

INGREDIENTS

- 1 pound lean ground beef
- 1 medium onion
- 3 cans minestrone soup
- 2 cans (10 ounces each) tomatoes with green chiles
- 1 can (10 ounces) diced tomatoes
- 1 can (28 ounces) baked beans
- 1 cup frozen corn kernels

DIRECTIONS

In large pot or Dutch oven over medium heat, brown beef and drain off grease.

Add onions and sauté until translucent. Add tomatoes, beans and corn. Simmer until hot and corn is cooked.

Top with sour cream and cheddar cheese, if desired.

Serve with peanut butter and jelly sandwich, saltine crackers or corn scoops.

This makes a big pot full. Leftovers can easily be frozen and taste just as good as fresh made.

This stew is especially good to take frozen on camping trips with or without horses. I put it in the cooler beside other cooled items in lieu of ice. Serve a big bowlful and pull up beside the campfire.

Quick Beef Stew

Contributed by Susan Howe Wain

INGREDIENTS | SERVES 6

- 1½ pounds round steak (about ¾-inch thick)
- 3 tablespoons all-purpose flour
- 1 tablespoon salt
- ½ teaspoon pepper
- ¼ cup shortening
- 2 cups carrots, chopped in 1-inch chunks
- 2 large onions, sliced
- 1 large potato, cut in 1-inch cubes
- 1 cup sliced celery
- 1 cup sliced mushrooms
- 1 bay leaf
- 3 cups water
- 1 cup sour cream
- 2 teaspoons paprika

DIRECTIONS

About 45 minutes before serving, cut meat into ¼-inch strips.

On waxed paper, combine salt, flour and pepper. Coat meat and reserve remaining flour mixture.

In large skillet over medium-high heat, brown floured meat well in melted shortening. Add carrots, onions, potato, celery, mushrooms, bay leaf and 3 cups water. Simmer, covered, over medium heat for 30 minutes or until meat and vegetables are fork tender. Stir in remaining flour mixture and cook until thickened slightly, stirring constantly. Stir sour cream and paprika into stew. Heat, but do not boil.

Photo: Courtesy of Susan Howe Wain

Greek Beef Stew with Onions

Contributed by Danielle Veasy

INGREDIENTS | SERVES 8

2 pounds boneless beef bottom round, trimmed
1 tablespoon olive oil
1½ cups water, divided
3 medium onions, finely chopped
2 cloves garlic, minced
¼ teaspoon pepper
1 bay leaf
1 teaspoon sugar
½ teaspoon thyme
1 cinnamon stick (3 inches long)
1 can (8 ounces) tomato sauce
½ cup dry red wine
1 tablespoon red wine vinegar
Chopped parsley for garnish
⅓ to ½ cup feta cheese, crumbled

DIRECTIONS

Cut beef into 1-inch cubes.

In wide pan, combine beef, oil and ½ cup water. Cover and simmer 30 minutes.

Add onions, garlic and pepper. Cook, uncovered, 30-35 minutes, until most of the liquid has evaporated and onions are browned.

Blend in remaining 1 cup water. Add bay leaf, sugar, thyme, cinnamon stick, tomato sauce and wine. Cover and simmer 1½ hours. Stir in vinegar and salt to taste. Garnish with parsley and cheese.

Liner Chili

Contributed by Wade and Ceci Liner

INGREDIENTS | SERVES 15

3 pounds lean ground beef
Salt and pepper
1 tablespoon olive oil
2 large onions, chopped
10 cloves garlic, minced
7 fresh jalapenos, stemmed, seeded, and minced
1 tablespoon red wine vinegar
1 can (28 ounces) whole tomatoes with juice
1 can (28 ounces) diced tomatoes with juice
1 can (6 ounces) tomato paste (optional)
1 can (16 ounces) kidney beans, rinsed and drained
1 can (16 ounces) great northern beans, rinsed and drained
1 can (16 ounces) pinto beans, rinsed and drained
6 tablespoons chili powder
2 tablespoons cumin
1 tablespoon ground black pepper

DIRECTIONS

In skillet, brown meat and season with salt and pepper. Place meat in large pot and set aside.

In large frying pan over medium high heat, combine oil, onions, garlic and peppers, and cook until vegetables are softened, 6-8 minutes, before adding to large pot.

Add remaining ingredients and water or dark beer to pot and cover. Simmer for about 3 hours. Optional toppings include grated cheese, sour cream, chopped onions, corn chips and chopped jalapenos.

This chili is hot, but cooks can make a milder version by reducing the number of jalapenos and spices. The recipe comes from Wade's grandparents. We served it at our hunt breakfast and it certainly warmed people up.

Bubbe's Favorite Brisket Recipe

Contributed by Susan, Maya and Bob Montani

INGREDIENTS

2½ pound brisket
Salt and pepper
Flour for dusting
1 onion, chopped
3 cloves garlic
2 tablespoons olive oil
Baby carrots, cut in halves or quarters
Bliss or fingerling potatoes, cut in halves or quarters
1 can tomato sauce
¼ cup dark brown sugar
1 small can cranberry sauce
¼ cup ketchup

DIRECTIONS

Preheat oven to 325 F.

Sprinkle brisket with salt and pepper, then flour brisket.

Sauté onion and garlic in oil. Add brisket and brown both sides.

In medium saucepan, mix tomato sauce, sugar, cranberry sauce and ketchup, and heat thoroughly over low temperature.

Put brisket in oven dish, fat-side down. Cover entire brisket with sauce. Top with carrots and potatoes. Cover with foil. Cook 3-3 ½ hours.

This is a dish our family always makes for holidays, which always includes a ride first!

Eye of Round with Gingersnaps

Contributed by Danielle Veasy

INGREDIENTS | SERVES 6-8

½ cup ketchup
1½ cups water
2 tablespoons sugar
2 tablespoons cider vinegar
2 tablespoons horseradish
2 tablespoons Worcestershire sauce
2 teaspoons dry mustard
½ teaspoon salt
½ teaspoon ground allspice
¼ teaspoon pepper
1 large onion, chopped
1 bay leaf
1 beef eye of round roast (1 ½ to 2 pounds), trimmed
⅓ cup crushed gingersnaps
3 to 4 cups cooked egg noodles
Parsley, chopped

DIRECTIONS

In large bowl, combine ketchup, ½ cup water, sugar, vinegar, horseradish, Worcestershire sauce, mustard, salt, allspice, pepper, onion and bay leaf. Add roast. Cover and refrigerate 8 or more hours.

Transfer roast and marinade to a heavy pan. Stir in remaining water. Bring liquid to boil. Reduce heat, cover and simmer 3 hours. Transfer meat to a platter.

Skim and discard fat from cooking liquid. Stir in gingersnaps and bring to boil. Cook, stirring, until crumbs are dissolved and sauce has thickened.

Slice roast and spoon on gingersnap sauce. Serve with noodles. Garnish with parsley.

Photo: Courtesy of Moore County Historical Association Collection, Southern Pines, NC

Dick and Reggie's Meatloaf

Contributed by Dick Moore

INGREDIENTS | SERVES 10

1 cup chopped celery
1 cup chopped onion
Olive oil for sautéing
2 pounds ground sirloin
½ pound ground pork
½ pound ground veal
1½ cups bread crumbs
½ cup parsley
⅓ cup sour cream
1 egg
1 tablespoon Worcestershire sauce
1 teaspoon marjoram
1 teaspoon thyme
Salt and pepper
Browning and Seasoning sauce
1 bottle chili sauce or ketchup

DIRECTIONS

Preheat oven to 350 F.

In skillet, sauté onion and celery in oil until tender.

Mix meats. Add celery and onion mixture, breadcrumbs, parsley, sour cream, egg, Worcestershire sauce, marjoram and thyme. Add salt and pepper to taste. Mix well.

Form into loaf and place in baking pan.

Rub with browning sauce and cover with chili sauce or ketchup. Bake 1-1 ½ hours.

Sometime in the mid-1990s, Reggie Miller had an idea for a party to be held at his Half Pond Farm. He wanted to invite some of the ladies of horse country for a Mother's Day dinner. He asked me to be his partner and I agreed. We entertained a group of about 50, including spouses. This is our recipe for the main course. The party was such a success that we had another 50 guests for Father's Day, one month later.

Marinated Flank Steak

Contributed by Sherry Mortenson

INGREDIENTS

1 flank steak
⅓ cup soy sauce
⅓ cup Worcestershire Sauce
⅓ cup balsamic vinegar

DIRECTIONS

Place sauces and vinegar in large zip-close bag and turn occasionally.

Score flank steaks on both sides and put in zip-close bag with marinade overnight.

Grill about 6 minutes on each side. Slice diagonally and serve.

Really good cold on buttered toast the next day.

Marinated Beef Tenderloin

Contributed by Jane Simon

INGREDIENTS | SERVES 8

1 cup Port wine
1 cup soy sauce
½ cup olive oil
1 teaspoon dried thyme
½ teaspoon hot sauce
4 cloves garlic, minced
1 bay leaf
5 pounds beef tenderloin, trimmed and tied

DIRECTIONS

In large roaster, combine Port wine, soy sauce, olive oil, thyme, hot sauce, garlic and bay leaf. Add beef. Cover and chill 8 hours, turning occasionally.

Preheat oven to 425 F.

Remove beef from marinade. Discard marinade. Place beef on rack in roasting pan.

Bake for about 40-50 minutes or until desired degree of doneness.

May keep heat at 140 degrees for the perfect medium after standing.

Cover and let stand at least 10 minutes before slicing.

Photo: Courtesy of Jeanne Paine

Marinated Beef on a Stick

Contributed by Danielle Veasy

INGREDIENTS | SERVES 6

- ½ pound boneless top sirloin steak, trimmed
- ½ cup soy sauce
- 1 tablespoon oil
- 2 tablespoons honey
- 2 tablespoons red wine vinegar
- 1 clove garlic, minced
- ¼ teaspoon pepper
- ½ teaspoon ground ginger

DIRECTIONS

Partially freeze steak for 30-45 minutes. Cut steak across grain into ¼-inch thick by 4-inch long slices.

Combine steak, soy sauce, oil, honey, vinegar, garlic, pepper and ginger. Mix well. Cover and refrigerate 1-2 hours.

Remove meat from marinade. Weave strips onto thin skewers so meat lies flat. Place on lightly greased grill, 4-6 inches above hot coals. Cook 4-5 minutes, brushing often with marinade and turning once.

Midwest Sunday Pot Roast

Contributed by Lynn Harvey

INGREDIENTS

- 2½-4 pound boneless beef chuck roast, thawed or still frozen
- 1½ tablespoons salt
- 3 cups water
- 6-7 whole carrots
- 1 large or 2 medium onions, cut into 6 wedges
- 4-6 gold potatoes, with skins

DIRECTIONS

Preheat oven to 275 F.

Place roast in roasting pan. Rub salt onto roast. Add water.

Cook 7 hours. Two hours before end of cooking time, flip roast and add carrots, onions and potatoes. Serve with gravy.

This roast is fork tender, falls apart, and melts in your mouth. For a Prairie Home Companion Sunday dinner, serve with red gelatin.

82 | MOORE COUNTY HORSE COUNTRY COOKING

Photo: Courtesy of Moore County Hounds

Bobotie

Contributed by George Manley

INGREDIENTS | SERVES 6

Cold water
2 slices white bread
2 onions, chopped
2 tablespoons butter
2 cloves garlic, crushed
1 ¼ pounds lean ground beef
2 tablespoons madras curry paste
1 teaspoon dried mixed herbs
3 cloves
5 allspice berries
2 tablespoons peach or mango chutney
3 tablespoons raisins
6 bay leaves
1 teaspoon salt and pepper to taste
1 ¼ cups whole milk
2 large eggs
Salt and pepper to taste

DIRECTIONS

Heat oven to 350 F.

Pour cold water over bread and set aside to soak.

Fry onions in butter for 10 minutes, stirring continuously. Add garlic and beef, and stir well. Stir in curry paste, herbs, spices, chutney, raisins, 2 bay leaves, 1 teaspoon salt and plenty of ground black pepper. Cover and simmer 10 minutes.

Squeeze water from bread. Beat bread into meat mixture until well blended then place in oval 9-by-5-by-3-inch baking dish. Press mixture down well and smooth top. Can make this and keep chilled a day ahead.

For topping, beat milk and eggs with salt and pepper to taste. Pour over meat. Top with remaining 4 bay leaves and bake 35-40 minutes or until topping is set and golden.

A traditional South African dish.

Photo: Courtesy of Monika Bargmann Brown

Hamburger Stroganoff

Contributed by Monika Bargmann Brown

INGREDIENTS | SERVES 4

- 2 large (or 3-4 small) shallots, diced
- 1 pound cremini or baby bella mushrooms, diced
- 8 ounces small bowtie noodles
- 1 tablespoon olive oil
- 1 pound ground sirloin
- 2-3 bags stroganoff mix
- 1 teaspoon thyme
- 1-2 teaspoons ground nutmeg
- Ground pepper
- 1 can (10.5 ounces) beef consommé
- 1 onion, chopped
- ½-⅔ cup sherry
- 1-2 teaspoons ketchup
- ¼ cup sour cream

DIRECTIONS

In nonstick saucepan, brown shallots and mushrooms (keep firm) in a little butter. Set aside and keep warm.

In boiling water, cook bowtie noodles partially, about 5 minutes. Drain and set aside.

Heat olive oil; add ground sirloin, stroganoff mix and spices. Brown meat, stirring frequently. Add stock, onions, sherry and ketchup. Cook, stirring, about 5 minutes. Taste and add more stroganoff mix or water if needed.

Stir in partially cooked noodles and simmer a few minutes, allowing noodles to absorb moisture. Serve quickly, and add sour cream and a little more sherry just before serving.

Adapted from a recipe by Margaret Menuez Brown.

Wild Rice Baron

Contributed by Mary Strasser

INGREDIENTS | SERVES 12-16

- 2 cups raw wild rice
- 4 cups water
- 2 teaspoons salt
- 2 pounds lean ground beef
- 1 pound fresh mushrooms
- 1 cup chopped onion
- ½ cup chopped celery
- ½ cup butter
- ¼ cup soy sauce
- 2 cups sour cream
- 1 ½ teaspoons salt
- ¼ teaspoon pepper

DIRECTIONS

Preheat oven to 350 F.

In a large covered pan over medium heat, gently cook rice in water with salt for 1 hour. Drain. Brown ground beef.

Rinse mushrooms, cut off tips of stems, slice caps, and saute, in butter, with onions and celery for five minutes.

Combine soy sauce, sour cream, salt and pepper. Add cooked rice, beef, onion, mushrooms and celery. Toss lightly and place in greased 3-quart baking dish. Bake for about 1 hour, uncovered. Add water if needed and season to taste. Stir several times during baking.

Recipe freezes well.

Hunting hounds look pleadingly and howl at visitors approaching their fenced compound in Horse Country. Excitable foxhounds are pack animals, and huge numbers are kept for the chase.

Photo: Courtesy of Moore County Historical Association Collection, Southern Pines, NC

La Bamba

Contributed by Sally Stetson

INGREDIENTS | SERVES 6

- 1 cup chopped onion
- 1 cup chopped peppers
- 1 cup fresh spinach
- 2 pounds ground beef
- 1 can (15 ounces) tomato sauce
- 1 cup frozen or drained, canned corn
- 2 cans (16 ounces each) low-fat refried beans
- 2 cups shredded sharp cheddar cheese

DIRECTIONS

Preheat oven to 350 F.

In skillet, brown onions and peppers with ground beef. Add spinach. Cook until spinach wilts, then drain. Add tomato sauce.

Place meat mixture into bottom of 9-by-13-inch baking pan.

Layer corn over meat, then refried beans. Shave an ample layer of sharp cheddar cheese over beans.

Bake 45 minutes until bubbly and hot.

Yum. Total crowd pleaser. Great leftovers too!

Elk Burgers

Contributed by Lynn Harvey

INGREDIENTS | SERVES 12-16

- 20 ounces ground elk (from Earth Fare in Raleigh, North Carolina)
- Celtic sea salt and pepper to taste
- 2 tablespoons light-tasting olive oil
- 1 heirloom or vine-ripened tomato, sliced
- Iceberg or Bibb lettuce
- Onion rolls

DIRECTIONS

Form ground elk into four 4-ounce patties. Season with salt and pepper to taste.

In nonstick pan, add olive oil and fry on medium heat until browned on both sides. When juices run clear, burgers are done. Serve on sliced onion rolls with lettuce, tomato and favorite condiments.

Tip: Don't try to grill elk because it's a very low-fat game and gets too dry.

Photo: Courtesy of Moore County Historical Association Collection, Southern Pines, NC

Osso Buco

Contributed by Stephen Later

INGREDIENTS | SERVES 4

4 veal shanks

Marinade
5 green olives
5 calamata olives
6 cloves garlic
1 sprig rosemary
10 leaves lemon verbena
Juice of ½ lemon
¼ Vidalia onion
1 Roma tomato
2 tablespoons pignoli nuts
½ teaspoon oregano
¾ teaspoons kosher salt
½ teaspoon ground pepper
1 teaspoon parsley
½ teaspoon chives
1 shiitake mushroom
½ cup olive oil
½ cup apple cider vinegar
¼ cup red wine vinegar
1 tablespoon balsamic vinegar

DIRECTIONS

Combine marinade ingredients. Marinate shanks overnight.

Roast in covered baking dish for 2 ½ hours at 325 F.

Serve topped with reduced marinade.

Fettuccine Alfredo

Contributed by Mary Strasser

INGREDIENTS

½ pint heavy cream
1 cup grated fresh Parmesan cheese
1 egg yolk
1-2 cloves garlic, minced
1 tablespoon chopped parsley
Salt and pepper to taste
1 pound fettuccine
1 stick butter

DIRECTIONS

In bowl, mix cream, cheese, egg yolk, garlic, parsley, salt and pepper.

Cook fettuccine al dente.

In large pot, melt butter. Remove from heat and mix butter and fettuccine. Add cheese mixture and stir.

Moroccan Lamb Tagine

Contributed by Lisa Taylor

INGREDIENTS | SERVES 6

½ teaspoon ground cinnamon
½ teaspoon ground cumin
½ teaspoon ground allspice
Salt to taste
Pepper to taste
Red pepper to taste
4-5 pounds lamb shoulder, trimmed and cut into ½-inch cubes
4 tablespoons extra virgin olive oil
1 large onion, chopped
4 cloves garlic, mashed, minced or pressed
½ cup white wine
2 medium sweet potatoes, peeled and cut into ½-inch chunks
2 medium carrots, cut on the bias into ½-inch chunks
4 tablespoons honey
4 tablespoons fresh lemon juice, reserving zest
½ cup chicken stock
Zest from fresh lemons
¼ cup white raisins or pitted prunes, snipped
Fresh cilantro
¼ cup chopped toasted almonds
Couscous, cooked (optional)

DIRECTIONS

In bowl, combine ¼ teaspoon of the following spices: cinnamon, cumin, allspice, salt, pepper and red pepper (reserving the other ½ teaspoon of each for later). Place lamb in bowl with spices and mix well.

In heavy-bottomed stew pot, heat olive oil until simmering. Brown spiced lamb in batches. Set aside.

Add a bit more oil to pan if needed. Cook onion in olive oil until translucent. Add garlic.

Add remaining ¼ teaspoon of the following spices: cinnamon, cumin, allspice, salt, pepper and pinch of red pepper to the pan to bloom. Stir well. Do not let burn.

Deglaze pan with the wine. Stir up the brown bits, cooking off most of wine.

Return lamb to the pot along with sweet potatoes, carrots, honey, lemon juice and chicken stock. Bring to a simmer. Adjust seasoning for salt and a balance of lemon and honey.

Bring to boil, then reduce to a very low simmer. Cover and simmer 40 minutes (30 minutes if you plan to reheat).

Add lemon zest, raisins or prunes just before serving.

Top with fresh chopped cilantro and chopped toasted almonds. If in season, fresh pomegranate seeds are an excellent accompaniment. Ladle stew over hot couscous.

This North African stew is ideal for entertaining because it's best made the day before so flavors can further develop. Gently reheat before serving. I serve it over couscous with naan. It is deceptively simple to prepare and wonderfully complex in flavor.

Pork Tenderloin with Honey Mustard and Orange Slices

Contributed by Marcia Bryant

INGREDIENTS | SERVES 6-8

½ teaspoon kosher salt
½ teaspoon black pepper
½ teaspoon garlic powder
2 pounds pork tenderloin
2 tablespoons extra virgin olive oil
2 tablespoons spicy mustard
2 tablespoons local honey
2 tablespoons orange juice
¼ teaspoon ground ginger
2 naval oranges
1 lemon

DIRECTIONS

Preheat oven to 375 F.

In bowl, mix salt, pepper and garlic powder.

Brush meat with about 1 tablespoon oil and rub on spice mixture.

In heavy skillet over medium-high heat, remaining oil. When skillet is hot, brown meat. When brown, turn over and cook an additional 1-2 minutes. Remove from heat.

Thinly slice one orange and arrange layered slices on top of tenderloin.

Mix together mustard, honey, orange juice and ginger. Spoon mix over meat and bake 30 minutes or until meat temperature reaches 150 F.

Remove meat from oven and squeeze juice from lemon over meat. Let stand at least 5 minutes, then slice into 1-inch thick slices. Place a slice or two of orange on the plate, then pork slices, and top with a spoonful of pan juices.

Photo: Courtesy of Moore County Historical Association Collection, Southern Pines, NC

Desserts

Photo: Courtesy of Leigh Virtue

Light Chocolate Chip Cookies

Contributed by Kathy Virtue

INGREDIENTS
2 ½ cups flour
1 teaspoon baking soda
¼ teaspoon salt
1 cup packed brown sugar
¾ sugar
½ cup butter, softened
1 teaspoon vanilla
2 large egg whites
¾ cup semisweet chocolate chips

DIRECTIONS
Preheat oven to 350 F.

Lightly spoon flour into dry measuring cup and level with knife. In bowl, whisk flour, baking soda and salt.

In large bowl, combine sugars and butter, and beat with a mixer at medium speed until well blended. Add vanilla and egg whites, and beat 1 minute. Add flour mixture, and beat until blended. Add chocolate chips and stir until mixed.

Drop dough by level tablespoons 2 inches apart onto 9-by-13-inch baking sheets coated with cooking spray.

Bake 10 minutes or until lightly browned. Cool on pans for 2 minutes, then remove and cool completely on wired racks.

Yellowframe Farm Cookies

Contributed by Barbara Tober

INGREDIENTS | YIELDS about 8 dozen

- 1 pound (4 sticks) lightly salted butter, room temperature
- 10 tablespoons sugar
- 2 teaspoons vanilla
- 4 cups all-purpose flour
- 4 cups pecans, finely ground
- 80-100 pecan halves
- 1 cup confectioners' sugar

DIRECTIONS

Preheat oven to 325 F.

In mixer, beat butter until creamy and almost white. Beat in sugar, one tablespoon at a time. Add vanilla.

Sift flour into butter mixture. Mix in ground pecans, 1 cup at a time. Beat 3-5 minutes.

Chill dough about 1 hour.

Form dough into 1½-inch balls. On baking sheet, press pecan half into each ball. Bake 15-20 minutes. Let cool for 5 minutes, then sift powdered sugar over top.

These have been served to many happy guests at Yellowframe Farm for decades.

Peanut Butter Surprise Cookies

Contributed by Jamie McDevitt

INGREDIENTS

- 2 ½ cups whole wheat pastry flour
- 2 teaspoons baking soda
- ¾ teaspoon sea salt
- 1 ½ cups sugar
- ½ cup coconut oil
- 1 cup peanut butter
- ¼ cup ice water
- 1 tablespoon molasses
- 1 teaspoon vanilla
- 2 cups potato chips, crushed slightly (surprise ingredient!)

DIRECTIONS

Preheat oven to 375 F.

Sift together flour, baking soda and salt. Set aside.

In mixer, combine sugar, coconut oil and peanut butter. Mix until creamy. Add water, molasses and vanilla. Mix well. Add flour mixture in 3 additions, mixing after each addition. Add potato chips, mixing until just combined.

Arrange 2 tablespoon-sized balls of cookie dough 2 inches apart on baking sheet lined with parchment. Press to about ¾-inch thick. Mark each cookie with crosshatch pattern using back of a fork. Bake 15 minutes. Cool. Then eat enough to make yourself sick!

Quick Oatmeal Cookies

Contributed by Elizabeth Rose

INGREDIENTS | YIELDS 24

½ cup butter
½ cup brown sugar, firmly packed
½ cup granulated sugar
1 egg
1 teaspoon vanilla
1 tablespoon milk
1 cup all-purpose flour
½ teaspoon baking soda
½ teaspoon baking powder
½ teaspoon salt
1 cup uncooked, quick-rolled oats
¾ cup chocolate chips

DIRECTIONS

Preheat oven to 350 F.

In mixer, cream butter and sugars.

In bowl, combine egg, vanilla and milk. Add to mixer. Beat until smooth.

Sift flour, baking soda, baking powder and salt. Add to mixer.

When beaten smooth, add oats and chocolate chips. Beat well.

Drop cookies 2 inches apart on a well-greased cookie sheet. Bake 10 minutes, until light brown.

Emeline Harvey's Christmas Sugar Cookies

Contributed by Lynn Harvey

INGREDIENTS

1 cup butter, softened to room temperature
1 ½ cups pure cane sugar
1 egg
1 teaspoon vanilla
2 ½ cups sifted flour
1 teaspoon cream of tartar
¼ teaspoon salt

DIRECTIONS

Preheat oven to 350 F.

In mixing bowl, cream butter and sugar by beating slightly. Slowly and gradually add sugar while beating until mixture is thoroughly mixed and fluffy. Add egg and vanilla. Beat well, about 1 minute on medium with electric mixer.

Gradually sift together all dry ingredients into creamed mixture while folding.

Divide dough. Use teaspoon to scoop out dough. Roll into 1-inch balls and place on an ungreased cookie sheet. Let sit for several minutes and flatten with a damp cloth over the bottom of a glass with a flat bottom.

Bake 10 minutes.

Charlotte Harvey's variation: Put a Hershey's kiss in the center of each cookie.

Photo: Courtesy of Moore County Historical Association Collection, Southern Pines, NC

Aunt Caroline's Nut Cookies

Contributed by Caroline Young

INGREDIENTS
- 1 stick butter
- 3 eggs
- 1½ cups flour
- 1 teaspoon baking powder
- 2 cups dark brown sugar
- 1 teaspoon salt
- 1 cup minced nuts
- 1 teaspoon vanilla

DIRECTIONS
Preheat oven to 350 F.

Melt butter. Beat eggs, then add flour, baking powder, sugar, butter, salt, nuts and vanilla. Spread batter in 10-by-15-inch heavy pan.

Bake about 8 minutes or until cake tester shows clear. Cut in squares.

Cookies are delicious hot or cold. My Aunt Caroline used to send me these. They are great!

Catharine Wain's Ginger Cookies

Contributed by Charlie Wain

INGREDIENTS
- ¾ cup shortening
- 1 cup sugar
- 2 eggs
- 5 cups flour
- 2 teaspoons baking soda
- 1 teaspoon cinnamon
- 1 teaspoon salt
- 2 teaspoons ginger
- ½ cup sour cream
- 1 cup molasses

DIRECTIONS
Preheat oven to 375 F.

Mix shortening with sugar. Add eggs.

Sift flour with soda, cinnamon, salt and ginger.

Add sour cream. Add molasses. Roll out and cut.

Bake 8 minutes.

Charlotte (Wentworth) Harvey's Chocolate Nut Clusters

Contributed by Lynn Harvey

INGREDIENTS

1 package (12 ounces, about 2 cups) milk chocolate chips or quality solid milk chocolate

1 cup unsalted, roasted almonds

1 cup unsalted, roasted jumbo cashews

DIRECTIONS

Line cookie sheets with wax paper. In double boiler over low heat, melt chocolate chips.

When chocolate is melted, remove top pan. Stir in nuts carefully so pieces don't break. Using a fork, drop clusters onto wax paper. Refrigerate 30 minutes until set.

Store, tightly covered, in refrigerator.

Dube's Scotcharoos

Contributed by Angie Tally

INGREDIENTS

1 cup sugar
1 cup light corn syrup
1 cup peanut butter
6 cups rice crisp cereal
6 ounces chocolate chips
6 ounces butterscotch chips

DIRECTIONS

In 3-quart saucepan over moderate heat, combine sugar and syrup, stirring frequently until mixture begins to bubble.

Stir in peanut butter and mix well. Add cereal and mix well. Press into buttered 9-by-12-inch pan.

In separate saucepan over low heat, melt chocolate and butterscotch bits, stirring occasionally. Spread over cereal mixture.

Refrigerate until chocolate sets. Cut into small squares to serve.

96 | MOORE COUNTY HORSE COUNTRY COOKING

Photo: Courtesy of Pam Jensen

Barbara (Harvey) Mentz's Caramel

Contributed by Lynn Harvey

INGREDIENTS

- 1 cup melted butter
- 1 can (14 ounces) sweetened condensed milk
- 1 cup corn syrup
- 2 cups brown sugar

DIRECTIONS

In medium saucepan, combine ingredients. Bring to boil, stirring occasionally, and boil to softball stage (232 F on a candy thermometer), then pour mixture into buttered, 9-by-13-inch pan and let cool. Once cool, cut into squares.

For popcorn balls: Prepare several squares of wax paper. Drizzle mixture over unsalted, air popped popcorn. Mix slightly with a plastic spoon so as not to break the kernels. Butter hands periodically and shape balls quickly. Wrap each one in wax paper.

Robert Harvey, Charlotte's son, warns to be careful when eating this caramel. It can pull the crowns right off your teeth while you're chewing.

Charlotte Harvey's Christmas Turtles

Contributed by Lynn Harvey

INGREDIENTS

- 1 bag (12 ounces) semisweet chocolate chips
- Pecan halves, roasted and unsalted

DIRECTIONS

Make Barbara (Harvey) Mentz's Caramel (*see recipe*). Be sure caramel is made soft, but not runny.

In double boiler, melt semisweet chocolate chips or a good semisweet chocolate.

Use caramel squares or roll caramel in your hands into oval shapes. If you're creative, make legs.

Dip into melted chocolate. Place on wax paper lined cookie sheets.

Top with a roasted unsalted pecan half.

Cinnamon Brittle

Contributed by Lei Ryan

INGREDIENTS

- 1 package (4.8 ounces) cinnamon graham crackers
- 8 ounces chopped pecans
- 1 stick butter, melted
- 1 stick margarine
- ¼ cup brown sugar
- 1 teaspoon vanilla extract
- ¼ cup sugar

DIRECTIONS

Preheat over to 350 F.

Break graham crackers and place on foil-lined cookie sheet. Cover with chopped pecans.

In saucepan, combine butter, margarine, brown sugar, vanilla and sugar. Bring to boil, stirring continuously, for 3 minutes. Mixture will froth. Spread frothy mixture evenly over graham crackers and pecans.

Bake 10 minutes. Allow to cool. Refrigerate and break apart into pieces.

Cocoa Crackles

Contributed by Tara Butler

INGREDIENTS INGREDIENTS | YIELDS 3 ½ dozen

- ¾ cup all-purpose flour
- ½ cup whole wheat flour
- ⅓ cup unsweetened cocoa powder
- ½ teaspoon salt
- ½ teaspoon baking soda
- ½ cup (1 stick) butter, softened
- ½ cup granulated sugar
- ¼ cup light brown sugar, packed
- 2 eggs, lightly beaten
- 1 teaspoon vanilla
- 1 cup confectioners' sugar

DIRECTIONS

Preheat oven to 350 F.

Lightly grease two cookie sheets.

Combine flours, cocoa, salt and baking soda.

Beat butter, brown sugar and granulated sugar with an electric mixer. Add eggs and vanilla. Beat until well blended. Add flour mixture. Beat until just blended.

Make two heaping teaspoons full of dough into balls. Roll in confectioners' sugar until coated. Place coated balls 2 inches apart on cookie sheets. Bake 11 minutes or until cookies are set and no longer shiny. Let cool 2 minutes before transferring to racks to cool.

Milk Chocolate Toffee Bars

Contributed by Tara Butler

INGREDIENTS

- ½ cup unsalted butter, softened
- 1 cup light brown sugar, packed
- 1 large egg, at room temperature
- 2 teaspoons vanilla
- 1 ¼ cups unbleached all-purpose flour
- 1 teaspoon baking powder
- ¼ teaspoon salt
- ½ cup milk chocolate chips
- ½ cup toffee baking bits

DIRECTIONS

Preheat oven to 350 F.

Mold a piece of foil into a square, 8-inch baking pan, leaving an inch overhang of foil to fold over edges. Lightly butter foil.

In bowl, beat butter and sugar until well blended and smooth. Add egg and vanilla, beating until well blended.

In separate bowl, whisk flour, baking powder and salt. Add to butter mixture and beat on low until almost blended. Add chocolate chips and toffee bits. Beat until evenly blended. Scrape dough into prepared pan. Smooth the top.

Bake 35-40 minutes. Cool completely before removing from pan. Remove by lifting up opposite foil edges. Peel off foil. Cut bars into desired size for desired yield.

Charlotte Harvey's Christmas Whipped Cream Balls

Contributed by Lynn Harvey

INGREDIENTS

- 1 ¼ pounds (20 dry ounces) "dipping" chocolate/milk chocolate
- 1 cup heavy whipping cream (best without food additives)
- Nuts, finely chopped (pecans or almonds)

DIRECTIONS

In large saucepan, melt chocolate over medium heat. Cool until thickened, but still able to be stirred. Add whipping cream. Mix thoroughly. Cover and chill in refrigerator until solid.

Using a spoon, roll into small balls. Roll balls in finely chopped nuts until completely covered.

MOORE COUNTY HORSE COUNTRY COOKING

Photo: Courtesy of Landon Russell

Molasses Crinkles
Contributed by Deborah Wilson

INGREDIENTS | YIELDS 4 dozen

- ¾ cup shortening, softened
- 1 cup brown sugar
- 1 egg
- ¼ cup molasses
- 2 ¼ cups flour
- 2 teaspoons baking soda
- ¼ teaspoon cloves
- 1 teaspoon cinnamon
- 1 teaspoon ginger

DIRECTIONS

In bowl, thoroughly mix shortening, sugar, egg and molasses.

Measure flour by dip-level-pour method or by sifting. Blend in soda, cloves, cinnamon and ginger.

Mix dry and wet ingredients. Chill.

Heat oven to 375 F.

Roll into balls the size of large walnuts. Dip tops... Place balls, sugared side up, 3 inches apart on baking sheet. Sprinkle each with 2 or 3 drops of... 12 minutes.

...her, Norma Bundy, while growing up in the

Honey Jam Bars
Contributed by Marcia Bryant

INGREDIENTS | YIELDS 2 ½ dozen

- ½ cup butter
- ½ cup honey
- 1 ½ cups flour, sifted
- 1 teaspoon baking powder
- 1 teaspoon cinnamon
- ½ teaspoon salt (optional)
- ¼ teaspoon nutmeg
- ¼ teaspoon all spice
- 1 egg, beaten
- ¾ cup jam

DIRECTIONS

Preheat oven to 400 F.

In bowl, cream butter and add honey. Blend well. Add sifted dry ingredients and mix. Add beaten egg.

Spread half the batter in a greased pan and spread with jam. Cover jam with remaining batter.

Bake 30-35 minutes. Cut into 1-by-3-inch bars.

Black and White Brownies

Contributed by Leslie and John Watschke

INGREDIENTS

2 tablespoons unsalted butter, plus 8 tablespoons
8 ounces white chocolate pieces
2 large eggs, lightly beaten
½ cup sugar
1 cup flour
½ teaspoon pure vanilla extract
½ teaspoon baking powder
¼ teaspoon salt
½ cup pecan pieces
7 ounces semisweet chocolate, chopped
Powdered sugar for garnish

DIRECTIONS

Preheat oven to 350 F.

Grease an 8-inch square baking pan with 2 tablespoons butter.

In double boiler, melt remaining 8 tablespoons butter with white chocolate.

Whisk together eggs and sugar. Add flour, vanilla, baking powder and salt. Mix well. Fold in pecans and melted white chocolate.

Spread mixture in prepared pan and sprinkle with the chopped semisweet chocolate.

Bake 40-45 minutes. Allow to cool before cutting into squares. Sprinkle with powdered sugar before serving.

Life is seldom "black & white" but this Black and White Brownie recipe is sure to please, whether or not you have a black and white paint to ride in The Walthour-Moss Foundation to work off the calories that sadly come with them. It's worth it – both brownies and the ride through the foundation on a horse of any color.

Photo: Courtesy of Terry Cook

Barbara (Harvey) Mentz's Apple or Rhubarb Crisp

Contributed by Lynn Harvey

INGREDIENTS

- 1 cup butter
- 2 cups flour
- 2 cups sugar, divided
- ½ cup oatmeal
- 5 cups sliced apples or diced rhubarb
- 1 teaspoon cinnamon
- 2 tablespoon corn starch
- 1 cup water

DIRECTIONS

Preheat oven to 350F.

Mix butter, flour, 1 cup sugar and oatmeal for crust. Pat bottom of greased, 9-by-13-inch pan, but reserve 1 cup for top layer.

[...]ps of fresh sliced apples or rhubarb over crust [...]

Combine 1 cup sugar, cinnamon, cornstarch [...] til thick and syrupy. Pour mixture over [...] crust. Sprinkle saved crust over

Lemon Lush

Contributed by Terry Cook

INGREDIENTS

- 2 sticks butter
- 2 cups flour
- 1 cup crushed walnuts
- 8 ounces cream cheese
- 1 cup confectioners' sugar
- 1 cup whipped cream
- 2 packages (3.4 ounces each) instant lemon pudding
- 3 cups milk

DIRECTIONS

Preheat oven to 350 F.

In bowl, cut butter into flour and mix with nuts. Press into 9-by-13-inch pan. Bake 20-25 minutes. Cool.

In separate bowl, beat cream cheese with sugar. Fold in whipped cream. Spread on crust.

In large bowl, mix pudding with milk. Beat until smooth. Spread on top of cream cheese mixture.

Top pudding with whipped cream.

You can use chocolate pudding for a Chocolate Lush.

Orange Blossoms
Contributed by Jane Simon

INGREDIENTS | YIELDS 24 large, 48 small, or 60 very small cakes

Orange Dip
Juice of 2 oranges
Juice of 2 lemons
Grated rind of 1 orange
1 ¼ pounds confectioners' sugar

Cake Batter
1 ½ cups flour
½ teaspoons salt
1 ½ teaspoons baking powder
3 eggs
1 ⅓ cups sugar
½ cup water
1 teaspoon vanilla

DIRECTIONS

Orange Dip
Combine juices and rind. Sift in sugar. Mix until smooth.

Cake Batter
Make orange dip first. Preheat oven to 350 F.

Sift together flour, salt, and baking powder three times. Set aside.

Beat eggs until creamy. Add sugar.

Add dry ingredients and water alternately to the egg and sugar mixture, beginning with the water. Add vanilla. Mix well. Pour batter into two greased and floured 12-18 cup muffin pans.

Bake 12 -15 minutes, depending on muffin size.

Remove from pans and dip while hot in orange dip. Place on wax paper to cool. Store in tin box. Do not refrigerate. Freezes nicely.

Fruit Flan
Contributed by Joan Hilsman

INGREDIENTS

Crust
1 cup flour
¼ cup sugar
½ cup cold butter
1 egg yolk
¼ teaspoon vanilla

Filling
8 ounces cream cheese

⅓ cup sour cream
⅓ cup sugar
½ teaspoon vanilla

Topping
Strawberries, grapes, kiwi, peaches, blueberries or any fruit

DIRECTIONS
Preheat oven to 400 F.

In food processor or pastry blender, mix flour, sugar and butter until mixture is well combined with pea-sized butter pieces. Stir in egg and vanilla. Mix with a fork and then with hands until well blended. Press into flan pan with removable bottom. Bake 15-20 minutes. Cool.

In large bowl, beat cream cheese, sour cream, sugar and vanilla. Spread into cooled crust. Cover top of flan with fruit decoratively arranged. Chill.

Impressive, yet easy.

MOORE COUNTY HORSE COUNTRY COOKING

Photo: Courtesy of Moore County Historical Association Collection, Southern Pines, NC

Sunny's Fruit Dip

Contributed by Angie Tally

INGREDIENTS

1 can (8.5 ounces) cream of coconut
1 large package (8 ounces) cream cheese
1 tablespoon pineapple juice

DIRECTIONS

In blender, combine ingredients.

Use all your favorites fruits to dip

Old Fashioned Honey Sauce on Fruit

Contributed by Marcia Bryant

INGREDIENTS

½ cup butter
⅔ cup local honey
2 tablespoons flour
2 eggs beaten lightly
½ cup lemon juice
½ pint whipping cream, whipped

DIRECTIONS

In double boiler, mix butter, honey, flour and eggs. Cook until thickened.

Remove from heat. Add lemon juice. Mix thoroughly, then let cool. When ready to serve, fold in whipped cream.

This is also good over gingerbread and pound cake.

Photo: Courtesy of Jeanne Paine

Pineapple Casserole

Contributed by Andrea C. Moore

INGREDIENTS | SERVES 6-8

- 2 cans (15.25 ounces each) pineapple chunks or tidbits, drained
- 7 slices white bread, cubed with crust removed
- 8 tablespoons butter or margarine, softened
- 1 cup sugar
- 4 eggs, slightly beaten
- 1 teaspoon vanilla

DIRECTIONS

Preheat oven to 350 F.

Pour drained pineapple over cubed bread. Set aside.

Cream butter and sugar. Add eggs and vanilla.

Pour over bread and pineapple, and mix well.

Pour into 2-quart baking dish and bake 50 minutes to 1 hour, or until top is brown and knife inserted in center comes out clean.

Kerstin's Apple Delight

Contributed by Gindy and William White

INGREDIENTS

- ¾ cup flour*
- 2 eggs
- ¾ cup sugar
- 1 teaspoon baking powder
- Dash salt
- 10 apples, pared, cored and sliced (amount as needed)
- ½ cup (1 stick butter), thinly sliced
- 1 tablespoon sugar

DIRECTIONS

Preheat oven to 375 F. Grease a square, 9-by-9 inch baking pan.

In bowl, combine flour, eggs, sugar, baking powder and salt. Pat into prepared pan.

Place enough apples to fill entire pan (apples can be substituted by other fruits, like fresh blueberries or raspberries).

Sprinkle with butter and sugar. Bake 30-40 minutes.

For making this recipe gluten free, use Pamela's baking mix and leave out baking powder.

We lived in Southern Pines many years ago and enjoyed the trails, jumps and foxhunting. Here is a great recipe a Swedish friend shared several years ago. So easy and good!

Apple Brown Betty

Contributed by Deborah Wilson

INGREDIENTS | SERVES 6

- ½ to 1 cup sugar*
- ¼ teaspoon cinnamon
- ¼ teaspoon nutmeg
- ¼ teaspoon salt
- 1½ cup soft breadcrumbs
- 3 cups sliced or chopped apples
- ¼ cup water
- Juice and grated rind of 1 lemon
- 3 tablespoons butter

DIRECTIONS

Preheat oven to 350 F.

Mix sugar, cinnamon, nutmeg and salt. *If apples are very tart, use additional sugar, up to 1 cup.*

Place ⅓ breadcrumbs and 1½ cups apples into greased, 1½-quart baking dish. Sprinkle with ½ of sugar mixture. Repeat.

Mix water, lemon juice and rind. Pour over apple mixture. Add remaining breadcrumbs and dot with butter. Cover and bake 1¾ hours.

Can use rhubarb, peaches, pineapple, bananas or cherries instead of apples.

All Star Tartlets

Contributed by Wanda Little

INGREDIENTS

- 36 frozen mini phyllo pastry shells
- ⅓ cup semisweet chocolate chips
- 1 cup finely chopped toasted pecans
- ¾ cup light brown sugar, packed
- 1 tablespoon butter, softened
- ¼ cup bourbon
- 1 large egg, lightly beaten

DIRECTIONS

Preheat oven to 350 F.

Arrange shells on a lightly greased cookie sheet.

Sprinkle chocolate chips into shells. In bowl, combine pecans, sugar, butter, bourbon and beaten egg.

Spoon evenly into shells.

Bake 20 minutes or until golden brown.

Blackberry Cobbler

Contributed by Deborah Wilson

INGREDIENTS

3 cups blackberries
1½ cups sugar, divided
¾ cup flour
2 teaspoons baking powder
¾ cup milk
Pinch of salt
1 stick butter, melted

DIRECTIONS

Preheat oven to 350 F.

Combine blackberries and 1 cup sugar. Set aside.

With spoon, mix ½ cup sugar, flour, baking powder, milk and salt.

Pour mixture on top of melted butter. Dot around and add blackberries. Do not stir.

Bake 1 hour.

Chocolate Tart

Contributed by Linda Selbach

INGREDIENTS | SERVES 12-16

1½ cups gingersnap crumbs
6 tablespoons butter, melted
3 tablespoons confectioners' sugar
1¾ cups heavy cream
15 ounces bittersweet or semisweet chocolate
1 teaspoon vanilla extract
Whipped cream (optional)

DIRECTIONS

Preheat oven to 350 F.

Stir together gingersnap crumbs, butter and confectioners' sugar. Firmly press onto bottom and sides of 9-by-9-inch baking pan. Bake 8-9 minutes or until fragrant. Let cool for 30 minutes.

In 3-quart saucepan over medium high heat, bring cream to boil.

Process chocolate in food processor or blender until finely ground. With processor running, pour in hot cream and vanilla in a slow steady stream. Process until smooth.

Pour mixture into cooled crust. Chill, uncovered, 3 hours. Garnish with whipped cream if desired.

Chocolate Irish Coffee Mousse

Contributed by Tara Butler

INGREDIENTS

2 ½ cups heavy cream, divided
2 teaspoons instant coffee
6 tablespoons sugar, divided
Dash salt
8 ounces dark chocolate, finely chopped
6 tablespoons Irish Cream liquor

DIRECTIONS

In small saucepan, combine ¼ cup heavy cream, coffee powder, 3 tablespoons sugar and salt. Bring to boil, then remove from heat. Add chocolate. Allow to cool 1 minute, then stir until smooth. Add liquor and set aside. Cool to room temperature.

Beat remaining 2¼ cups heavy cream until soft peaks form. Add 3-4 tablespoons sugar, one at a time, until cream is stiff. Set aside 1 cup of whipped cream for garnish.

Fold remaining whipped cream in three parts into the slightly cooled chocolate mixture. Spoon into espresso cups or custard cups. Cover with plastic wrap and chill at least 2 hours.

Garnish with a dollop of the reserved whipped cream and a chocolate covered espresso bean or chocolate shavings.

Chocolate Pot de Crème

Contributed by Effie Ellis

INGREDIENTS | SERVES 4

1 cup milk
12 ounces dark chocolate
1 egg
1 egg yolk
Pinch salt
1 tablespoon brandy
1 teaspoon vanilla extract

DIRECTIONS

Heat milk but do not boil.

In blender, mix chocolate, egg, egg yolk, salt, brandy and vanilla.

Add heated milk in blender and mix 1 minute.

Pour into small ceramic containers and chill in refrigerator.

Photo: Courtesy of Susan, Maya and Bob Montani

Eartha Morrison's Chocolate Chip Dessert

Contributed by Susan Howe Wain

INGREDIENTS | SERVES 8

15 graham crackers
¼ cup (½ stick) butter, melted
30 marshmallows
½ cup milk
1 cup whipping cream
1 square bitter chocolate, chipped

DIRECTIONS

Crush crackers and add melted butter. Line a pie tin with mixture, leaving a little for the topping.

Melt marshmallows with milk and allow to cool, but not stiff. Add whipped cream and chipped chocolate.

Pour into pie tin and refrigerate.

Easy Dirt Dessert

Contributed by Susan and Maya Montani

INGREDIENTS | SERVES many

1 ¼ pounds chocolate sandwich cookies
8 ounces cream cheese, softened
1 cup confectioners' sugar
½ cup melted butter
2-3 cups milk
12 ounces whipped cream
1 teaspoon vanilla
2 small packages of French Vanilla Instant Pudding Mix

DIRECTIONS

Crumble cookies in food processor (or crush and mince with a rolling pin in a plastic bag). Reserve some cookies for topping.

Mix together cream cheese and confectioners' sugar. Add butter, milk, whipped cream, vanilla and instant pudding, and mix.

Layer cookie crumbs and cream cheese mixture until ingredients are gone and top with cookies. Chill.

This is a favorite of the Eno Triangle Pony Club and all the teens at the Chapel Hill Equestrian barn too (as well as the parents). You'll find this dessert at our potluck gatherings.

Mary Elsner Mielke's Mince Meat

Contributed by Lynn Harvey

INGREDIENTS

Mincemeat
- 3 pounds young venison or lean beef, cooked in slow cooker until tender
- 1 gallon apple cider, boiled down to 2 quarts
- 2 pounds brown sugar
- 2 cups sour cherry preserves or reconstituted dried Michigan cherries
- 1 tablespoon cinnamon
- ½ teaspoon cloves
- 1 tablespoon salt
- 1 cup meat juice
- 22 ounces currants
- 45 ounces raisins
- 9 large apples peeled and chopped (Wealthy or Courtland apples are best. Other varieties that work are Honey Crisp or Mountaineer.)
- 3 tablespoons ground orange rind and lemon rind, mixed
- 1 teaspoon nutmeg
- 2 teaspoons mace
- ¼ cup butter

Pie Recipe
- 2 cups mincemeat
- 2 large apples (see mincemeat ingredients for varieties), peeled and sliced thinly
- ⅓ cups apple juice
- 2 tablespoons butter
- 2 tablespoons brandy
- 1 unbaked pie shell (9 inch)

DIRECTIONS

Mincemeat

Grind cooked meat. Combine with remaining ingredients and simmer gently until apples are tender. Stir occasionally.

Pour hot into sterilized pint jars and process in pressure cooker for 20 minutes at 10 pounds pressure. Or place in large 14-ounce freezer containers and freeze.

Pie

Preheat oven to 350 F.

In bowl, combine mincemeat, apples and apple juice. Dot with butter and brandy over top, then place over crust. Bake 35-45 minutes.

This recipe was handed down to my great grandmother, Mary (Elsner) Mielke.

Photo: Courtesy of Landon Russell

Pumpkin Cupcakes

Contributed by Carol Butler

INGREDIENTS
- 1 package (15.25 ounces) spice cake mix
- 1 can pure pumpkin
- 3 large eggs
- ⅓ cup vegetable oil
- ⅓ cup water

DIRECTIONS
Preheat oven to 350 F.

In mixing bowl, combine cake mix, pumpkin, eggs, oil and water, and beat 2 minutes.

Pour batter ¾ full into 24 muffin cups with paper liners. Bake 16-21 minutes.

Ice with cream cheese icing.

Quick and easy!

Big Irene's Lemon Cupcakes

Contributed by Landon Russell

INGREDIENTS

Cake
- 1 package (15.25 ounces) white or yellow cake mix
- 1 package (3.4 ounces) lemon instant pudding
- ¾ cup water
- ¾ cup vegetable oil
- Juice and rind of one lemon
- 4 eggs

Glaze
- ½ pound powdered sugar
- Juice and rind of 3 lemons

DIRECTIONS
Preheat oven to 350 F.

In bowl, mix cake ingredients. Bake in well greased 1 ½ -inch cupcake tins for 6 minutes. Lower oven temperature to 300 F and bake for an additional 6 minutes.

While cake is baking, combine sugar, lemon juice and lemon rind in bowl. Remove cupcakes immediately from tins and dip in glaze. Set dipped cakes on cake rack to cool.

A treasured and favorite recipe from my grandmother, Irene Hilliard.

Too Many Eggs Angel Food Cake

Contributed by Katie Walsh

INGREDIENTS | SERVES 10

1¼ cups flour, sifted
¼ teaspoon salt
1 cup sugar, plus ½ cup
2 cups egg whites (about 15 eggs)
1¼ teaspoons cream of tartar
1 teaspoon vanilla extract

DIRECTIONS

Preheat oven to 325 F.

Sift flour, salt and ½ cup sugar.

Beat egg whites until bubbly. Add cream of tartar. Continue beating egg whites until fluffy and smooth. Sprinkle in remaining cup of sugar, 1 tablespoon at a time, while beating. Continue beating until egg whites hold curled peaks. Beat in vanilla.

With spatula, carefully fold in flour mixture in four batches, until flour barely disappears.

Scrape batter into ungreased 10-inch tube pan. Run a table knife through batter to remove air pockets.

Bake 40 minutes, until golden and firm.

Turn tube pan upside down over a wine bottle. Let cake cool this way for at least 1 hour.

Run a table knife around edge of tube pan. Turn cake onto serving plate.

Many horse country residents raise their own chickens. In the summer months, when hens lay prolifically, this is a great recipe to use all those eggs. I serve it with fresh crushed fruit in juices and whipped cream.

Cold Oven Pound Cake

Contributed by Meredith Mannheim

INGREDIENTS | SERVES 12-16

3 cups flour (measured after sifting 3 times)
1 cup (2 sticks) butter, softened
½ cup shortening
3 cups sugar
5 eggs, room temperature
1 cup milk
1 teaspoon vanilla
½ teaspoon baking powder
½ teaspoon salt

DIRECTIONS

Grease a Bundt pan well with shortening or cooking spray.

Sift and measure flour.

Cream butter, shortening and sugar. Add eggs and beat well. Add milk, then flour and beat well. Add vanilla, baking powder and salt.

Pour batter into Bundt pan. Put in cold oven and set to bake at 325 F for 1½ hours.

Let cake cool 5-10 minutes before removing from pan.

This cake has been made in my family at least as far back as my great grandmother. I can't remember a family function, trip to the beach, welcoming new neighbors or cookouts without this Cold Oven Pound Cake. Of course, as a child my job was to lick the spoon and beaters. But now, being the fourth generation to make it, I will whip it up at a moment's notice. The smell of it baking is amazing (and I've even used that when trying to sell a house). I believe one of the best ways to enjoy it is what my husband does to it. David will cut a couple of slices and toast them in the oven with butter. Then he meets me in the truck as we haul the horses down to The Walthour-Moss Foundation for Opening Hunt with the Moore County Hounds. There is no better way to start off Thanksgiving Day than that!

German Chocolate Cake

Contributed by Bonnie Caie

INGREDIENTS | SERVES 12-16

1½ cups granulated sugar
1 cup butter, softened
4 large eggs
2¼ cups flour
1½ teaspoons baking soda
¼ teaspoon salt
1 cup sour cream
½ cup milk
¾ teaspoons vanilla extract
4 ounces sweet baking chocolate, melted

Topping

¾ cup evaporated milk
½ cup light brown sugar, firmly packed
½ cup butter
3½ ounce can flaked coconut
1 cup chopped pecans

DIRECTIONS

Preheat oven to 350 F.

Grease and flour two round 9-inch baking pans.

In mixer, combine sugar and butter. Add eggs and mix. Add flour, baking soda, salt, sour cream, milk, vanilla and melted chocolate. Mix.

Pour mixture into baking pans. Bake 35 minutes. Cake is done when tester comes out clean. Cool in pans 10 minutes, then place on wire racks for 20 minutes.

Topping

In bowl, mix milk, brown sugar, butter, coconut and pecans.

Using a thread to split layers in two, creating 4 layers. Place cake on serving dish with topping between layers, saving adequate topping for top layer (*sometimes I double the topping recipe*).

I've served this to the horse community, and my German friends are particularly impressed!

Pony Treat Cake
Contributed by Kelly Rossi

INGREDIENTS
1 cup sugar
1 cup light brown sugar
1 cup flour (or gluten-free flour with xantham gum)
1 cup ground flax seed
1 teaspoon baking powder
1 teaspoon baking soda
1 teaspoon cinnamon
½ teaspoon ground ginger
½ teaspoon ground nutmeg
3 cups carrots, grated
1 ½ cups applesauce
4 eggs
2 teaspoons vanilla
½ cup of molasses
Butter or non-stick spray

DIRECTIONS
Preheat oven to 325 F.

Grease 9-by-13-inch cake pan with butter or nonstick spray.

In bowl, mix dry ingredients, and then add carrots, applesauce, eggs and vanilla. Beat until smooth. Pour into pan. Bake about 1 hour or until a knife comes out clean.

This is the perfect cake for you and your horse to enjoy together. Decorate with apple slices and drizzle with the molasses. This cake is traditionally iced with cream cheese icing, but that can be a bit much if you are sharing it with your horse.

Nana's Carrot Cake
Contributed by Elaine Zelch

INGREDIENTS
2 cups sugar
1 ½ cups canola oil
4 eggs
2 cups flour
2 teaspoons baking soda
1 teaspoon salt
3 teaspoons cinnamon
2 teaspoons vanilla
3 cups grated carrots

Cream Cheese Icing
1 stick butter
8 ounces cream cheese
4 cups confectioners' sugar
2 teaspoons vanilla

DIRECTIONS
Preheat oven to 325 F.

In bowl, combine sugar and oil. Add eggs. Sift flour, soda, salt and cinnamon together. Add to sugar mixture and beat well. Add vanilla and grated carrots. Bake in three well-greased, 8-inch layer cake pans. Can also use a rectangular pan. Bake 45 minutes. Once cool, ice with cream cheese icing.

Cream Cheese Icing
Soften butter and cream cheese and beat together. Add confectioners' sugar and vanilla until mixture reaches spreading consistency. Frost cake.

Photo: Courtesy of Charlene Pierce

Sharon's Best Cheesecake

Contributed by Sharon Granito

INGREDIENTS

- ¼ cup flour
- 1 stick butter, room temperature
- 3 tablespoons sugar
- 4 packages (8 ounces each, 2 pounds total) cream cheese, softened
- 1 ½ cups sugar
- 4 eggs
- ½ cup heavy cream
- 2 tablespoons flour
- 1 ½ teaspoon vanilla

DIRECTIONS

Preheat oven to 350 F.

To make crust, mix flour, butter and sugar. Press into 9-inch spring form pan. Bake 18-20 minutes. Top will be golden. Set aside to cool.

While crust is baking, in mixer, blend cream cheese and 1½ cups sugar. Add eggs one at a time while mixing. Add heavy cream, flour and vanilla, and mix.

Pour cheese mixture onto baked crust in spring form pan. Bake about 1 hour. Top will crack.

Gooey Butter Cake

Contributed by Charlene Pierce

INGREDIENTS

- 1 package (15.25 ounces) yellow butter cake mix
- 1 stick of butter, melted
- 4 eggs, divided
- 1 box confectioners' sugar, plus more for decorating
- 1 large package (8 ounces) cream cheese
- 1 teaspoon vanilla

DIRECTIONS

Preheat oven to 350 F.

In bowl, mix cake mix, butter and 2 eggs. Spread on well-greased pan (cookie sheet).

In separate bowl, mix confectioners' sugar, cream cheese, 2 eggs and vanilla. Spread on top of first mixture.

Bake 30 minutes.

Sprinkle with confectioners' sugar.

Flour-less Chocolate Fire Cake

Contributed by Devon Burnore

INGREDIENTS | YIELDS 10 to 12 squares

- 10 ounces semisweet chocolate, roughly chopped
- 7 tablespoons unsalted butter, cut into pieces
- 5 large eggs, room temperature
- 1 cup sugar
- Pinch of salt
- ¾ teaspoon cinnamon
- ¼ teaspoon ground ginger
- ¾ teaspoon ancho chili powder
- 1 tablespoon crushed red pepper
- ⅛ teaspoon ground habanero pepper
- Confectioners' sugar for dusting (optional)
- Cream cheese icing (optional)

DIRECTIONS

Preheat oven to 350 F.

Line the bottom of a 9 ½-inch springform pan with a circle of parchment paper.

Grease sides and parchment with butter or nonstick cooking spray.

In double boiler, melt chocolate and butter, stirring occasionally until smooth.

In large bowl, whisk eggs and sugar. Slowly, a bit at a time, whisk in melted chocolate. Add salt and spices to taste, adjusting spices if needed.

Pour into springform pan and bake 22-25 minutes or until toothpick comes out clean. Let cake cool completely on a wire rack. Ice with cream cheese icing or dust with confectioners' sugar and serve.

This cake will warm you up after a cold day of hunting.

Peach Blueberry Cake

Contributed by Anne Huberth

INGREDIENTS

Pastry
- 1 ½ cup flour
- ½ cup sugar
- 1 teaspoon baking powder
- ¼ teaspoon salt
- 1 stick (½ cup) cold, unsalted butter, cut into cubes
- 1 large egg
- 1 teaspoon vanilla

Filling
- ½ cup sugar
- 2 tablespoons flour
- 1 or more tablespoons quick cooking Tapioca
- 2 pounds ripe peaches (about 4), quartered, peeled, pitted and each quarter cut into quarters
- 1 cup blueberries (½ pint)
- 1 tablespoon fresh lemon juice

DIRECTIONS

Pastry
In food processor, together flour, sugar, baking powder and salt.

Add butter and pulse until mixture resembles coarse corn meal.

Add egg and vanilla, pulsing until dough forms.

Press dough into bottom and sides of pan(s). Chill until firm, about 10 minutes.

Filling
Preheat oven to 335 F.

Grind two tablespoons sugar with flour and tapioca until powdery. Transfer to large bowl and add in remaining 6 tablespoons sugar.

Add peaches, blueberries, and lemon juice. Toss gently to coat. Spoon filling into pan and bake loosely covered with a piece of tin foil. Bake until filling is bubbling and golden, and crust is golden, about 1 ½ hours.

Transfer cake to rack and cool uncovered 10 minutes.
Run spatula around side of pan, then carefully remove side of pan.

Perfect for peach season! Can be served plain at room temperature or garnish with whipped cream or vanilla ice cream.

Shaker Lemon Pie

Contributed by Oren Leblang

INGREDIENTS | SERVES 8

3 lemons, must be Meyer lemons
1 cup sugar
¼ teaspoon salt
4 eggs
3 tablespoons all-purpose flour
4 tablespoons butter, melted
1 egg white (optional)
Coarse sugar, for sprinkling (optional)
Dough for one double-crust pie

DIRECTIONS

Thoroughly wash and dry lemons. Finely grate all lemon zest into a bowl. With very sharp knife, slice lemons paper thin, removing seeds.

In glass bowl, layer slices and zest and sprinkle each layer with sugar and very light salt. Massage gently. Cover and set aside at room temperature for 24 hours to soften slices.

Preheat oven to 425 F.

Roll out pie crusts.

In bowl, lightly whisk eggs, adding flour, then melted butter until smooth.

Gently mix softened lemon-sugar mixture with eggs, melted butter and flour until well combined. Pour into prepared pie shell. Place top crust over filling and crimp edges. Cut slits in crust for venting.

Optional: Beat 1 egg white until frothy and brush over pie crust. Sprinkle with coarse sugar.

Bake 25 minutes in middle of oven.. Reduce temperature to 350 F and bake an additional 20-25 minutes, or until crust is golden.

Let pie cool on a rack and serve warm.

An unexpected delight! Meyer lemons are a necessity. Use regular lemons only for people you never want to talk to again, ever. Meyers lemons are sweeter but only available in season (November-March). Enjoy after a fish entrée, and then again for breakfast the next morning. The recipe is easy after meticulous work prepping the lemons.

Photo: Courtesy of Moore County Historical Association Collection, Southern Pines, NC

Bob Little's Favorite Pumpkin Pie with a Healthy Non Bullet-Proof Crust

Contributed by Lynn Harvey

INGREDIENTS

Crust
1 cup unsifted all-purpose flour, plus 2 tablespoons
2 tablespoons sugar
1/8 teaspoon salt
6-7 tablespoons organic shortening, room temperature
1 tablespoon bottled lemon juice, cold
1-2 tablespoons ice cold water

Filling
1 cup pure cane sugar
1 tablespoon ground cinnamon
1 teaspoon ginger
1/4 teaspoon cloves
2 large eggs
1 can (15 ounces) pure pumpkin
1 can (12 ounces) evaporated whole milk

Whipped Cream Topping
1 pint refrigerated heavy whipping cream
3 tablespoons pure can sugar
1 teaspoon vanilla extract

Secrets Your Mama Forgot to Tell You
- Lemon juice tenderizes crust.
- Cold water prevents flour from getting pasty (bakes tough).
- The more one handles pie crust the tougher it gets because the gluten in the flour is developed (think French bread).
- A foil crust guard prevents the edge of the crust from burning.
- Refrigerating dough causes steam to rise out of the crust, making it flakey.
- Buttered piecrusts burn very easily.

DIRECTIONS

Crust
In bowl, combine flour, sugar and salt. Add shortening. Cut fat into flour with fork. Be sure lumps are small and dispersed throughout flour. If any of the flour doesn't have lumps (smaller than pea size), add additional tablespoon of shortening.

In separate bowl, mix lemon juice with water. Sprinkle into flour and fat, 1 teaspoon at a time. Use hands to see if dough holds together in a ball. If not, open ball with fork and sprinkle in 1/2 of the last tablespoon. Repeat and add last 1/2 tablespoon of liquid. Press into a ball. *Warning: Do nothing else or crust gets bullet proof.*

Wrap in wax paper and refrigerate for at least 1 hour.

Filling
Preheat oven to 350 F.

Beat ingredients with mixer until thoroughly blended, about 1-2 minutes. Roll out chilled dough onto wax paper and flatten as much as possible with hands, squeezing cracks together. Top dough with a second sheet of wax paper. Roll out from center. Squeeze outer cracks together and flatten thicker area in center by pushing it evenly outward with a rolling pin.

Peel top sheet of wax paper off dough. Place upside down in pie pan and peel second layer off.

Shape into 9-inch pie pan without stretching. Roll edges under. Trim if necessary. Add flute by pinching thumb and forefinger together on outside of pan. From inside of pan, insert left forefinger between thumb and forefinger of opposite hand and pinch. Flour hands lightly if necessary. Put back into refrigerator to keep cold, about 10 minutes.

Pour pumpkin filling into chilled crust until just below fluting. Cut strips of heavy-duty foil at least 16 inches long. Attach two ends together to make a long strip. Wrap around crust and attach into a seam with multiple folds on other end. Tighten and bend over the crust and pie, but not so it dips into filling.

Bake 1 hour. Test center of pie with toothpick. If toothpick doesn't come out clean, bake 10 more minutes and retest. Let cool. Remove foil when cool.

Whipped Cream Topping
Beat ingredients with mixer on high until soft peaks form. Serve immediately.

Deep Dish Pear Pie

Contributed by Edith Overly

INGREDIENTS | SERVES 6

6 large pears, peeled and sliced
½ cup sugar
½ teaspoon cinnamon
½ teaspoon nutmeg
2 tablespoons flour
½ cup butter
3 tablespoons lemon juice
1 unbaked deep-dish pie shell (9 inch)

DIRECTIONS

Select pears that are not too ripe. Place briefly in boiling water, then cold water to make peeling easier.

Butter baking dish. Slice pears into dish alternately with sugar, spices, flour, lemon juice and remaining butter. Cover with pastry crust. Slash crust in a few places.

Bake on the lower shelf 45-50 minutes or until pears are tender and syrup is caramelized.

If crust browns too quickly, cover with foil. Serve warm with cold whipped cream flavored with a little sugar and a drop of kirsch.

Photo: Courtesy of Andrea Chisholm

Barbara (Harvey) Mentz's Blueberry Nectar Pie

Contributed by Lynn Harvey

INGREDIENTS

6 cups blueberries, fresh
3 ¼ tablespoons softened tapioca
⅔ cup pure cane sugar
¼ teaspoon salt
1 ½ tablespoons lemon juice
½ cup brown sugar
1 ½ tablespoons butter, room temperature

DIRECTIONS

Preheat oven to 350 F.

In bowl, mix blueberries, tapioca, white sugar, salt and lemon juice. Fill unbaked piecrust (no fork holes) with berries. Sprinkle with brown sugar and dot with butter.

Place top crust on, flute and cut vents. Place foil collars around edges.

Bake 1 hour or until a few faint golden patches and liquid is translucent.

Lainer's Apple Crumb Pie

Contributed by Elaine Zelch

INGREDIENTS

5 to 7 Granny Smith Apples (about 5 cups)
Juice of ½ lemon
½ cup sugar
1 teaspoon cinnamon
½ cup sugar
¾ cups enriched flour
⅓ cup butter
1 unbaked pastry shell (9 inch)

DIRECTIONS

Preheat oven to 400 F.

Pare apples and cut in eighths. Remove seeds and squeeze lemon juice over apples to prevent discoloration. Mix ½ cup sugar and cinnamon, and sprinkle over apples. Arrange apples in unbaked pastry shell.

Mix ½ cup sugar and flour. Cut in butter until crumbly. Sprinkle over apples. Bake about 40 minutes. Cool. Spoon on whipped cream or ice cream.

Photo: Courtesy of Effie Ellis

LaVerne Harvey's Old Fashioned Apple Cream Pie

Contributed by Lynn Harvey

INGREDIENTS
5 cups McIntosh apples, peeled
1 ½ cups sugar
½ teaspoon salt
2 tablespoons cornstarch
2 eggs, beaten
1 cup heavy whipping cream
1 teaspoon vanilla
1 unbaked pie shell (9 inch)
Unbaked pie shell dough (enough for top of pie)

DIRECTIONS
Preheat oven to 350 F.

Cut apples into sixths, then thinly slice. Be sure slices are close in thickness or pie will be applesauce and raw pieces. Combine with remaining ingredients and place mixture in an unbaked pie shell. Roll out top crust and cover apples. Press together and flute. Cut vents into top crust.

Glaze crust with a beaten egg white thinned with 1 tablespoon water. Surround with foil collar. Bake 60-70 minutes. Pie will be done when crust has golden areas and liquid seeping through steam vents looks thickened.

Variation
This is a strange pie and has an acquired taste. For regular apple pie, skip the cream, add only 1 cup sugar, 2 tablespoons cornstarch or 3 tablespoons flour, and 1 ½ tablespoons cinnamon.

Photo: Courtesy of Moore County Historical Association Collection, Southern Pines, NC

My Mother's Deep Dish Apple Pie

Contributed by Shellie Sommerson

INGREDIENTS | SERVES 9

Pastry
1 cup flour
½ teaspoon salt
⅓ plus 1 tablespoon shortening
3 tablespoons cold water

Filling
1 ½ cups sugar
½ cup flour
1 teaspoon nutmeg
1 teaspoon cinnamon
¼ teaspoon salt
12 cups apples, pared and thinly sliced
2 tablespoons butter

DIRECTIONS

Preheat oven to 425 F.

In bowl, measure 1 cup flour and ½ teaspoon salt. Cut in shortening. Sprinkle in cold water, 1 tablespoon at a time, mixing until all flour is moistened and dough almost cleans the side of the bowl (add additional water 1 teaspoon at a time if needed).

Gather dough into ball. Shape into flattened square on floured surface. Roll dough into a 10-inch square. Fold in half and cut slits near center. Set aside.

In separate bowl, combine sugar, flour, nutmeg, cinnamon and salt. Mix with apples.

Turn into ungreased 9-by-2-inch baking pan and dot with butter. Unfold pastry over fruit. Fold edges under just inside edge of pan.

Bake 1 hour or until juice begins to bubble through slits in crust. Best served warm.

Pictured is Dave Kelly on horse
Photo: Courtesy of Kerry McCashin Batty

Meme's Pecan Pie
Contributed by Angie Tally

INGREDIENTS
- ½ cup brown sugar
- 3 tablespoons all purpose flour
- ¼ teaspoons salt
- 2 tablespoons butter
- ½ teaspoon vanilla
- 1 cup corn syrup
- 1 cup chopped pecans
- 1 prepared pie crust (9 inch)

DIRECTIONS
Preheat oven to 350 F.

In bowl, mix brown sugar, flour and salt. Add butter, vanilla and syrup. Mix well. Add pecans. Pour in prepared pie crust. Place crust on cookie sheet and bake 45 minutes.

It seems most of our family's favorites are desserts and sweets. I suppose after dinner is the most relaxing, when the work is done and no one is quite ready to get up from the table.

Custard Bread Pudding
Contributed by Claire Rhodes

INGREDIENTS
- 1 quart milk, scalded
- 2 cups day-old bread, cubed
- ¼ teaspoon salt
- ½ cup sugar
- 3 eggs
- 3 tablespoons melted butter or margarine
- 1 teaspoon vanilla

DIRECTIONS
Preheat oven to 325 F.

In bowl, pour milk over bread cubes. Add salt and sugar.

In separate bowl, beat eggs. Add to bread mixture with butter and vanilla. Mix well. Pour into 1½-quart greased baking dish.

Set casserole in a pan. Pour hot water to within 1 inch of top. Bake 50-60 minutes until knife inserted near rim comes out clean.

Sugar Free Frozen Custard

Contributed by Lynn Harvey

INGREDIENTS
- 5 fresh eggs
- 1 pint heavy whipping cream
- 1 tablespoon vanilla
- 2 ½ -3 tablespoons light agave nectar

DIRECTIONS
Set up ice cream maker.

Version 1
In mixing bowl (not ice cream maker bowl), beat eggs. Add whipping cream, vanilla and agave nectar, in order, and stir thoroughly. Do not use mixer. Quickly pour into ice cream maker.

Version 2 (for the nervous)
Before pouring into ice cream mixer, heat mixture, less agave nectar, on low heat in saucepan (recommend double boiler) until slightly thickened (coats spoon). Remove from heat and let cool. Add agave nectar. Stir very thoroughly and then quickly add to ice cream maker.

Variations
Use 3-4 eggs and add your favorite fruit or reduce the number of eggs and add 2 tablespoons of cocoa powder.

This is a rich ice cream, I invented out of desperation. Version 1 with the raw eggs tastes better. You will not find this recipe anywhere else, and it's quick and easy to make.

Buttermilk Ice Cream

Contributed by Mandy Misner

INGREDIENTS
- 4 farm fresh eggs * see note
- 1 pint heavy cream
- 1 ½ cups buttermilk
- ⅛ teaspoons salt
- ⅓ to ½ cup (to taste) organic light brown sugar (may also use plain sugar)
- 1 or 2 teaspoons vanilla (or to taste) or scrape seeds from ½ of a vanilla bean

DIRECTIONS
In blender on medium high, combine ingredients for 1 minute or until sugar is dissolved and cream cheese is fully incorporated. If all ingredients are chilled, mixture can be placed in a 1 ½-quart electric ice cream freezer and churned until frozen, approximately 20-30 minutes. Otherwise chill ingredients before churning.

Additions: Fruits like bananas or strawberries may be added to blender but should be added after other ingredients are blended. After adding fruit, pulse blender a few times until fruit chunks are to desired size. Also note, water is not your friend when striving for a creamy ice cream.

Note: I used to make a "custard" by separating the eggs and cooking the yolks with cream and vanilla bean, then chilling the ingredients. Now I've adapted to the blender method because it is simple and delicious, leaving me more time to play with my horses!

Breads, Breakfast & Beverages

Photo: Courtesy of Moore County Historical Association Collection, Southern Pines, NC

Photo: Courtesy of Caroline Young

Zucchini Bread

Contributed by Caroline Young

INGREDIENTS | YIELDS 16 SERVINGS

1½ cups whole wheat flour
½ cup fructose
1 teaspoon baking powder
½ teaspoon baking soda
¼ teaspoon ground cinnamon
¼ teaspoon ground nutmeg
¼ teaspoon ground cloves
1 large egg
1 egg white
3 tablespoons canola oil
1¼ cups grated zucchini, well packed (about ½ pound)
½ cup crushed pineapple, drained

DIRECTIONS

Preheat oven to 350 F.

Spray 5-by-9-inch loaf pan with nonstick vegetable oil.

In large bowl, combine flour, baking powder, baking soda, cinnamon, nutmeg and cloves.

In separate bowl, combine egg, egg white, oil, zucchini and pineapple.

Add dry ingredients to wet, and mix just until moistened.

Pour into prepared loaf pan. Bake 50-60 minutes, or until toothpick inserted in center is clean.

Remove loaf from pan and cool for at least 30 minutes before slicing.

Cornbread

Contributed by Katie Walsh

INGREDIENTS | SERVES 12

2 cups cornmeal (stone ground preferable)
1 teaspoon salt
1 teaspoon baking soda
2 cups buttermilk
2 eggs, lightly beaten
2 tablespoons unsalted butter, melted

DIRECTIONS

Preheat oven to 450 F.

In medium bowl, combine cornmeal, salt and baking soda.

In separate bowl, combine buttermilk and eggs, then add to cornmeal mixture. Add melted butter and stir.

Pour batter into greased 10-inch iron skillet or 12-cup muffin tin. Bake until golden, about 20-25 minutes.

My grandmother, a great cook, never put sugar in cornbread. It's great with chili, stews and beans – just about all Southern cooking. Our chickens love the leftovers!

Pecan Mini-Muffins

Contributed by Wanda Little

INGREDIENTS | YIELDS 24 mini-muffins

1 cup firmly packed brown sugar
½ cup butter, melted
1 teaspoon vanilla extract
2 large eggs
1 cup chopped pecans
½ cup all-purpose flour

DIRECTIONS

Preheat oven to 375 F.

In bowl, combine sugar, butter, vanilla and eggs, beating with wire whisk until smooth. Stir in nuts and flour. Spoon batter into 1¾ - 2-inch muffin pans coated with cooking spray or paper liners. Fill until ⅛-inch from top.

Bake 12 minutes.

Corn Muffins

Contributed by Lisa Taylor

INGREDIENTS | YIELDS 12

1 cup all-purpose flour
1 cup stoneground yellow cornmeal
6 tablespoons sugar
1½ teaspoons baking powder
¼ teaspoons baking soda
½ teaspoon salt
1 cup buttermilk
3 tablespoons unsalted butter, melted and cooled
3 tablespoons corn oil
1 large egg and 1 large yolk
1 - 1⅓ cups corn kernels, fresh, frozen or canned

DIRECTIONS

Center rack in oven and preheat to 400 F.

Line muffin tin with paper muffin cups. Place muffin pan on 9-by-13-inch baking sheet.

In large bowl, whisk flour, cornmeal, sugar, baking powder, baking soda and salt.

In large glass measuring cup or separate bowl, whisk buttermilk, melted butter, oil, egg and yolk until well blended. Pour liquid ingredients over dry ingredients and gently, but quickly, stir to blend. Batter will be lumpy. Stir in corn kernels. Divide batter evenly among muffin cups.

Bake 15-18 minutes or until tops are golden and tester inserted in center of muffin comes out clean. Transfer pan to rack and cool 5 minutes before removing muffins from tins.

Eleanor Walker's Spoonbread

Contributed by Caroline Young

INGREDIENTS
1 cup yellow cornmeal
3 cups milk
2 tablespoons butter
1 teaspoon salt
1 teaspoon baking powder
2 eggs, beaten

DIRECTIONS
Preheat oven to 375 F.

In double boiler, combine cornmeal and milk.

Cook about 30 minutes until mixture is mush.

Stir in butter, salt and baking powder. Add beaten eggs slowly while stirring.

Fold into a greased casserole dish.

Bake 30 minutes.

Aunt Kitty's Biscuits

Contributed by Jane Simon

INGREDIENTS
1 package rapid rise yeast
2-3 tablespoons warm water
5 cups flour
5 tablespoons sugar
1 tablespoon baking powder
1 teaspoon salt
1 teaspoon soda
1 cup shortening
2 cups old-fashioned buttermilk

DIRECTIONS
In bowl, dissolve yeast in warm water. Let stand.

In separate bowl, sift flour, sugar, baking powder, salt and soda. Cut in shortening. Stir in yeast mixture and buttermilk.

Place in covered container in the refrigerator overnight.

Knead dough and roll out on floured board. Cut into biscuits (I use a shot glass to make small biscuits). Place on 9-by-13-inch baking sheet. Brush with melted butter and allow to rise for several hours in a warm place without a draft.

Preheat oven to 400 F.

Bake 18-20 minutes until golden brown. For small biscuits, bake 8-10 minutes.

These are a must at every holiday dinner!

MOORE COUNTY HORSE COUNTRY COOKING | 133

Amazing Cinnamon Rolls

Contributed by Carol Butler

INGREDIENTS | YIELDS 12

1 package (26.4 ounces) frozen biscuits
2 cups boiling water
1 package (6 ounces) dried apricots (can substitute with golden raisins)
All-purpose flour to sprinkle
¼ cup butter, softened
1 teaspoon cinnamon
¾ cup brown sugar, packed
½ cup chopped pecans, toasted
1 cup confectioners' sugar
3 tablespoons milk
½ teaspoon vanilla

DIRECTIONS

Preheat oven to 375 F.

Arrange frozen biscuits with sides touching on a lightly floured surface. Allow to thaw 30-40 minutes. Should still be cool to touch.

In boiling water, soak apricots 10 minutes. Drain and chop.

Sprinkle biscuits with flour. Press edges together and pat into a rectangle. Spread top with softened butter.

Combine cinnamon and brown sugar. Sprinkle over buttered biscuits. Top with chopped apricots (or raisins) and pecans.

Roll up dough, starting at the long end. Cut into 12, 1-inch slices. Place rolls into 10-inch cast iron skillet, 10-inch round cake pan or 9-inch square pan. Bake 35-40 minutes or until center rolls are golden brown and done.

Mix confectioners' sugar, milk, and vanilla for icing. Spread over rolls while still hot. Cool before serving.

Photo: Courtesy of Moore County Historical Association Collection, Southern Pines, NC

Colonel Ken Benway's Superior Donuts

Contributed by Dick Moore

INGREDIENTS
YIELDS about a dozen dounts and holes

- 2 tablespoons vegetable shortening
- ¾ cup sugar
- 4 egg yolks
- 3 ½ cups sifted all-purpose flour
- 4 teaspoons baking powder
- 1 ¼ teaspoons salt
- ½ teaspoon ground nutmeg
- ¾ teaspoon ground mace
- ⅛ teaspoon ground cinnamon
- 1 ½ cups whole milk

DIRECTIONS

In medium bowl, mix shortening, sugar and egg yolks.

In separate bowl, sift together flour, baking powder, salt and spices.

Stir liquid mixture alternately with 1 cup milk into second mixture, until dry ingredients are moistened. Handle dough as little as possible.

Roll dough to about ⅜-inch thickness on a floured, cloth covered surface. Let stand 15 minutes (can also make the night before and put in refrigerator overnight with a sheet of clear wrap spread on top to keep skin from forming). Cut doughnuts out with floured 2, 2 ½, or 3-inch doughnut cutter (can also use a 3-inch diameter water glass to cut the large circumference and a shot glass to cut the inner hole).

Meanwhile, heat 1½ inches of frying fat to 370 F. Fat is ready when doughnut center browns in about 1 minute. Keep temperature steady. Fry doughnuts in hot fat, turning carefully with a wooden spoon handle when the first crack appears. Continue cooking and turning until browned nicely. Total frying time is about 1½ minutes. Drain doughnuts on brown paper or paper towels.

Tip: Use a good thermometer that stays fixed in the oil.

Photo: Courtesy of Maureen Grippa

Pancake Recipe

Contributed by Maureen M. Grippa

INGREDIENTS | SERVES 4

- 1 cup whole-wheat flour
- ½ cup bran cereal
- 2 tablespoons brown sugar
- 1 teaspoon baking soda
- 1 teaspoon cinnamon
- ¼ teaspoon salt
- ¼ teaspoon nutmeg
- 1 egg
- 1¼ cups milk
- ⅓ cup mashed banana
- ⅓ cup nuts (walnuts, pecans or sunflower seeds)

DIRECTIONS

In mixing bowl, combine all ingredients.

Pour batter into greased frying pan and cook 4 minutes per side on medium heat.

Egg and Cheese Soufflé

Contributed by Mary Strasser

INGREDIENTS | SERVES 4

- Butter
- 25 thin slices of bread, crusts removed
- 20 slices sharp cheddar cheese, divided
- 11 eggs
- 3 ½ cups milk
- Seasoned salt to taste

DIRECTIONS

Butter 9-by-13-inch baking dish. Put layer of bread in bottom. Top with half of cheese. Repeat.

Beat eggs, milk and salt until well blended. Pour over bread and cheese. Cover tightly and refrigerate overnight.

Preheat oven to 350 F.

Bring to room temperature. Bake about 45 minutes or until top is brown and puffy. (You may add diced ham or cooked shrimp over each layer.)

Photo: Courtesy of Terry Cook

Overnight Breakfast Casserole

Contributed by Maureen M. Grippa

INGREDIENTS | SERVES 8-10

- 8 slices bread, cubed
- 1½ pounds ground sausage
- 1 cup shredded Monterey Jack cheese
- 1 cup shredded cheddar cheese
- 4 large eggs, beaten
- 2½ cups, plus ½ cup milk
- ¾ teaspoon dry mustard
- 1 can (10¾ ounces) cream of mushroom soup

DIRECTIONS

Brown sausage and drain.

Arrange bread in ungreased 13-by-9-inch baking pan. Add sausage, Monterey Jack cheese and cheddar cheese.

Beat eggs and mix with 2½ cups milk. Pour over bread, cheese and sausage.

Cover casserole with foil. Refrigerate overnight.

Preheat oven to 300 F.

Combine mustard, ½ cup milk and mushroom soup. Pour over casserole. Bake uncovered for 1½ hours.

Sausage Casserole

Contributed by Terry Cook

INGREDIENTS

- 1 pound hot sausage
- 1 pound sweet sausage
- 2 cups rice, cooked
- 6 cups rice cereal
- 2 small onions, chopped
- 1 pound shredded sharp cheddar cheese
- 4 eggs, lightly beaten
- 2 cans (10.5 ounces each) cream of celery soup
- ¼ cup milk

DIRECTIONS

Preheat oven to 350 F.

In pan, brown sausage and chopped onions. Add cooked rice to browned mixture. Set aside.

In 9-by-13-inch baking dish, layer sausage mixture, rice cereal and shredded cheese. Continue layering until ingredients are gone.

Mix eggs, soup and milk. Pour over layered ingredients in pan. Bake 40 minutes.

Variations: Use beef or pork, cream of chicken or cream of mushroom soups.

Pictured are Raymond Firestone and Virginia Moss
Photo: Courtesy of Moore County Historical Association Collection, Southern Pines, NC

Opening Meet Hunt Breakfast Glazed Ham

Contributed by Cynthia Peterson

INGREDIENTS

Spiral ham, heated or warmed
2 sticks butter
1 cup brown sugar
¼ cup molasses
¼ cup apple cider
¼ cup bourbon
1 teaspoon ground cinnamon

DIRECTIONS

In saucepan over medium heat, combine butter, sugar, molasses, cider, bourbon and cinnamon. Simmer 10 minutes until glaze is the consistency of syrup.

Pour or drizzle over warm ham. Cover with foil until ready to serve.

Instant Russian Tea

Contributed by Alice Cramer Glass

INGREDIENTS | YIELDS 5 ½ cups dry mix (50-55 cups of tea)

1 ¾ cups sugar
1 ¼ cup unsweetened instant tea
1 large jar (1 pound 11 ounces) powdered orange drink
3 packages (.67 ounces each) small sized lemonade mix
1 ½ teaspoons ground cloves
1 ½ teaspoons ground cinnamon

DIRECTIONS

In airtight container, mix sugar, tea, powered orange drink, lemonade mix, cloves and cinnamon.

To prepare, place 2 heaping teaspoons per cup, then pour in hot water and stir.

Nick's Mother's Egg Nog

Contributed by Nick Ellis

INGREDIENTS | YIELDS 4 ½ gallons

5 dozen eggs
5 pounds sugar, divided
2 fifths bourbon
2 fifth brandy
1 fifth light rum
5 quarts milk
5 quarts cream

DIRECTIONS

Separate egg yolks and whites.

Beat egg yolks. Add all but 1 cup of sugar while beating. Still beating, add liquors, gradually at first. Still beating, add milk and cream. Set aside.

Beat egg whites stiff with remaining cup of sugar. Fold into eggnog.

Let eggnog stand at least a week in a cool place.

Will keep three months in a cool place.

Made after Thanksgiving, it is perfect for Christmas.

Photo: Courtesy of Moore County Hounds

Shirl-a-rita

Contributed by Shirley Gaither

INGREDIENTS

4 fresh limes
1 orange
1 liter Jose Cuervo tequila gold
1 liter triple sec
½ liter Rose's Lime Juice

DIRECTIONS

Squeeze fresh lime and orange into a large plastic container with a pour spout. Mix together with tequila, triple sec and lime juice. Shake and place in freezer for 5 days.

Pours like a slushy. This is a perfect drink to relax and guaranteed to remove all soreness. Enjoy!

Peachy Punchy

Contributed by Leslie Baldwin

INGREDIENTS | SERVES 12-16

6-8 fresh ripe peaches
Powdered sugar
1 gallon Chablis wine, chilled
Myers dark rum

DIRECTIONS

Slice peaches into 6 to 8 slices each. Place in bowl and cover with rum and powdered sugar to taste. Marinate overnight. In 2 ½-gallon container or large punch bowl, combine chilled Chablis and marinated peach mixture. Serve chilled.

This is especially tasty at the end of a long, hot, dry, and dusty day at the horse show. Beware the potent peaches!

Opening Meet Hunt Breakfast Cranberry Mimosas

Contributed by Cynthia Peterson

INGREDIENTS

4 cups cranberry juice, chilled
4 cups no pulp orange juice, chilled
2 bottles sparkling white wine, chilled
Orange slices for garnish (optional)

DIRECTIONS

Mix ahead and pour from pitcher into champagne flutes.

Flaming Shamrock

Contributed by Mike Russell

INGREDIENTS | SERVES 1

3 ounces Bushmills Irish Whiskey, divided
2 teaspoons demerara sugar
6-7 ounces hot coffee, brewed strong
Fresh whipped cream for topping

DIRECTIONS

Place sugar in wine glass or goblet. Add whiskey, then add coffee. Top with fresh whipped cream.

In medium saucepan, heat 1 ounce of whiskey and set aflame when hot. Carefully ladle a spoonful onto each coffee. Wait until flame expires before drinking.

Tip: Dim lights to see flame on whiskey. Don't use a plastic ladle.

Photo: Courtesy of Moore County Historical Association Collection, Southern Pines, NC

In the 1940s or 1950s, Mickey Walsh, the Godfather of Stoneybrook, clears a seven-foot fence at a Southern Pines horse show with no bridle or saddle. He is riding Little Squire, owned by Audrey Kennedy, a Southern Pines resident who spearheaded such civic efforts as establishing a humane society and a branch of the American Red Cross. Before Walsh's interests turned to steeplechasing and training, he and Little Squire won big at Madison Square Garden horse shows. Although the Walsh family descendants have since sold the farm, another group of equestrian enthusiasts in Southern Pines and Pinehurst have formed an organization and are continuing the Stoneybrook Steeplechases at The Carolina Horse Park.

Horse Show Tailgating

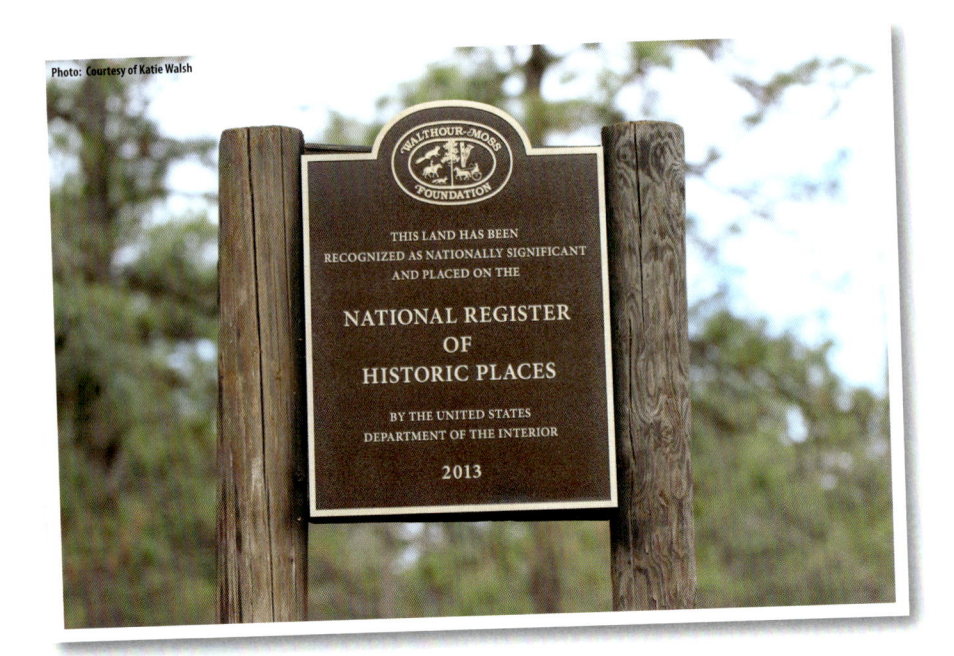

Potato Hash Cake

Contributed by Anne Huberth

INGREDIENTS

1 ⅓ pounds potatoes
2 tablespoons unsalted butter
1 cup fine bread crumbs
½ cup finely grated Parmesan cheese, plus 2 tablespoons
2 large eggs
6 ounces salami, finely chopped
6 ounces mozzarella, finely chopped
2 tablespoons chopped fresh parsley
1 clove garlic, minced
Pinch thyme
½ teaspoon salt and pepper to taste
3 tablespoons olive oil

DIRECTIONS

Peel potatoes and dice into ¼-inch cubes. Soak in cold water then drain.

In large pot over high heat, bring salted water to a boil and cook potatoes about 20 minutes, until tender. Drain and transfer to bowl.

Saute bread crumbs in butter until brown. Stir crumbs into potatoes with ½ cup parmesan, eggs, salami, mozzarella, parsley, garlic, thyme, and salt and pepper to taste.

In heavy cast iron 10-inch skillet, heat olive oil over medium heat. Press mixture into pan and brown. Add remaining two tablespoons Parmesan and bread crumbs on top. Place under broiler and brown.

Cool overnight.

This recipe can be made ahead. We took this to every Hunter Trials and Hunter Pace picnic. Slice into bite-sized squares and serve at room temperature.

Photo: Courtesy of Caroline Young

Black Bean Dip

Contributed by Joan Wilson

INGREDIENTS

- 1 can (15.25 ounces) black beans, rinsed and drained
- 1 can (11 ounces) shoe peg corn, drained
- 1 container (4 ounces) crumbled feta cheese (or chop a block)
- ¼ cup vegetable oil
- ¼ cup sugar
- ¼ cup apple cider vinegar

DIRECTIONS

In serving dish, combine ingredients and serve with tortilla chips.

An easy and very tasty dip recipe. Good for a crowd.

Caramel Corn

Contributed by Carol Butler

INGREDIENTS

- 7 quarts popped corn
- 2 cups dry roasted peanuts
- 2 cups brown sugar
- ½ cup light corn syrup
- 1 teaspoon salt
- 1 cup butter
- ½ teaspoon baking soda
- 1 teaspoon vanilla

DIRECTIONS

Preheat oven to 250 F.

Place corn and peanuts into two 9-by-13-inch shallow, greased baking pans.

In medium pan over high heat, combine brown sugar, corn syrup, salt and butter. Boil 5 minutes. Remove from heat and stir in baking soda and vanilla. Mixture will be light and foamy. Immediately pour over corn and peanuts. Stir to coat.

Bake 1 hour, removing each pan every 15 minutes to stir.

Line counter top with wax paper. Dump corn on wax paper to cool. Store in airtight container.

Photo: Courtesy of Effie Ellis

Shrimp and Mango Wraps

Contributed by Cathy Maready

INGREDIENTS | YIELDS 5 wraps

- ⅓ cup plain nonfat yogurt
- ⅓ cup light mayonnaise
- 1 tablespoon fresh chopped cilantro
- 1 tablespoon fresh lime juice
- Salt to taste
- Freshly ground pepper to taste
- 5 whole grain tortillas
- 2 cups fresh baby spinach
- 1 ripe mango, peeled and diced
- 1 ½ pounds cooked shrimp, peeled and deveined

DIRECTIONS

In blender or food processor, combine yogurt, mayonnaise, cilantro and lime juice. Pulse until smooth. Season to taste with salt and pepper. Refrigerate.

In small skillet over medium-high heat, warm tortillas (about 10 seconds per side). Arrange spinach in center of each tortilla. Top with mango and shrimp. Drizzle 2 tablespoons yogurt and mayonnaise mixture over each tortilla and roll up.

Pimiento Cheese

Contributed by Wayne Moore

INGREDIENTS

- 8 ounces cheddar cheese, shredded
- 8 ounces cream cheese, softened
- ½ cup mayonnaise
- ¼ cup sugar
- 1 small jar (4 ounces) diced pimiento, drained
- Jalapenos (optional)

DIRECTIONS

In blender, combine cheddar cheese and cream cheese. Add mayonnaise and sugar, and continue to mix. Stir in pimiento.

For a spicier version, add jalapenos, reduce mayonnaise, and use pepper and onion relish.

Broccoli Floret Salad

Contributed by Tammy Leber

INGREDIENTS | SERVES 6 or more

- 3-4 cloves garlic
- 1 ½ teaspoon salt
- 1 tablespoon prepared mustard
- ⅓ cup olive oil
- ¼ cup wine vinegar
- ½ cup Parmesan cheese
- 1 head broccoli, cut or 2 bags (14 ounces each) precut broccoli florets

DIRECTIONS

Smash garlic and salt into paste. In medium bowl, mix mustard, olive oil, vinegar and Parmesan cheese.

Add garlic and salt, then pour into gallon size zip-close bag.

Add broccoli florets to bag and shake.

Marinate 3-4 hours before serving.

This recipe begs for adaptation to make it your own. Add more or less salt, garlic, etc., to taste. I live on this during the summer, so I double the recipe to have more in the fridge.

Deviled Eggs

Contributed by Mary Ellen Bailey

INGREDIENTS

- 12 eggs
- ½ cup mayonnaise
- Salt and pepper to taste
- 1 tablespoon sugar
- 1- 1½ tablespoons Worcestershire sauce
- 1 cup sliced smoked salmon
- 2 tablespoons capers
- 2 tablespoons chives

DIRECTIONS

Boil and peel eggs. Slice lengthwise. Remove yolks and place in processor or mixer. Add enough mayonnaise to make the right consistency for filling egg whites. Add salt, pepper and sugar, then add Worcestershire sauce.

Place a small piece of smoked salmon on each egg, followed by yolk mixture.

With cake decorating sleeve, fill eggs over salmon. Top with capers and chives.

Photo: Courtesy of Moore County Historical Association Collection, Southern Pines, NC

Picnic Chicken

Contributed by Katie Walsh

INGREDIENTS | YIELDS 8 pieces

3½ to 4 pound chicken, cut into pieces
4 cloves garlic, pureed or pressed
½ cup heavy cream
¾ cup flour
1 stick (8 tablespoons) clarified butter
Salt and pepper

Clarified Butter

2 pounds unsalted, good quality butter, cut in cubes

DIRECTIONS

Preheat oven to 375 F.

Rub chicken with garlic. Season with salt and pepper. Refrigerate 15 minutes, uncovered.

Dip each piece of chicken in cream, then coat with flour. Let chicken pieces dry on a rack for 15 minutes.

Heat large skillet filled with ½-inch butter to medium-high heat. When hot, fry chicken pieces until golden brown on all sides, about 10 minutes.

Transfer chicken to rack placed over a baking sheet. Continue cooking in oven until chicken is done, about 30 minutes. Serve warm or cold.

Clarified Butter

In large pan on very low heat, warm butter until foaming stops. Use a slotted spoon to remove foam (save foam for seasoning vegetables).

Pour remaining butter through three layers of cheesecloth. Clarified butter will keep 3 months in the refrigerator.

Ham Biscuits

Contributed by Lisa Taylor

INGREDIENTS | SERVES 6

- 5 tablespoons salted butter, room temperature, divided
- 1 tablespoon fresh snipped chives, plus additional for topping
- 2 tablespoons Dijon mustard
- 1 package dinner rolls
- ¼ pound Black Forest ham, thinly sliced
- ¼ pound Gruyere or Swiss cheese, sliced

DIRECTIONS

Preheat oven to 350 F.

In mixing bowl, combine 4 tablespoons butter, chives and mustard.

Split rolls. It's preferable to keep entire sheet of rolls intact. Spread thin layer of mixture on both sides.

Layer ham and cheese on rolls. Replace tops. Spread tops of rolls with remaining tablespoon butter.

Wrap in foil. Bake about 20 minutes, until cheese is melted.

Snip fresh chives and sprinkle on rolls. Rewrap to keep warm.

Enjoy warm or at room temperature.

I love to cook and enjoy entertaining on a small scale, which includes my Lakebay neighbors and hosting my book club entirely comprised of horse country residents.

Index

APPETIZERS
Bacon Wrapped Crackers, 11
Baked Brie, 9
Betty Manness' Bourbon Hot Dogs, 18
Caviar Pie, 8
Cranberry Cheese Ball, 12
Empanadas Panamanian Canapé, 16
Hot Cheese Rounds, 9
Olé Olé, 8
Pineapple Chutney Appetizer, 19
Pizza Party Rounds, 16
Uncle Jim's Famous Water Chestnuts and Bacon, 10

BEEF
Bubbe's Favorite Brisket Recipe, 78
Bobotie, 83
Dick and Reggie's Meatloaf, 80
Emeline Harvey's Swedish Meatballs, 17
Eye of Round with Gingersnaps, 78
Hamburger Stroganoff, 84
La Bamba, 86
Marinated Beef on a Stick, 82
Marinated Beef Tenderloin, 81
Marinated Flank Steak, 80
Midwest Sunday Pot Roast, 82
Wild Rice Baron, 84

BEVERAGES
Flaming Shamrock, 141
Instant Russian Tea, 138
Nick's Mother's Egg Nog, 139
Opening Meet Hunt Breakfast Cranberry Mimosas, 141
Peachy Punchy, 140
Shirl-a-rita, 140

BREADS
Amazing Cinnamon Rolls, 134
Aunt Kitty's Biscuits, 133
Cornbread, 131
Corn Muffins, 132
Eleanor Walker's Spoonbread, 133
Pecan Mini-Muffins, 131
Zucchini Bread, 130

BREAKFAST & BRUNCH
Colonel Ken Benway's Superior Donuts, 135
Deviled Eggs, 147
Egg and Cheese Soufflé, 136
Overnight Breakfast Casserole, 137
Pancake Recipe, 136
Sausage Casserole, 137

CAKE & CUPCAKES
Big Irene's Lemon Cupcakes, 111
Cold Oven Pound Cake, 113
German Chocolate Cake, 114
Gooey Butter Cake, 116
Flour-less Chocolate Fire Cake, 117
Nana's Carrot Cake, 115
Peach Blueberry Cake, 118
Pony Treat Cake, 115
Pumpkin Cupcakes, 111
Sharon's Best Cheesecake, 116
Too Many Eggs Angel Food Cake, 112

CANDIES
Barbara (Harvey) Mentz's Caramel, 97
Caramel Corn, 145
Charlotte Harvey's Christmas Turtles, 97
Charlotte Harvey's Christmas Whipped Cream Balls, 99

COOKIES & BARS
Aunt Caroline's Nut Cookies, 95
Barbara (Harvey) Mentz's Apple or Rhubarb Crisp, 102
Black and White Brownies, 101
Catharine Wain's Ginger Cookies, 95
Charlotte (Wentworth) Harvey's Chocolate Nut Clusters, 96
Cinnamon Brittle, 98
Cocoa Crackles, 98
Dube's Scotcharoos, 96
Emeline Harvey's Christmas Sugar Cookies, 94
Honey Jam Bars, 100
Lemon Lush, 102
Light Chocolate Chip Cookies, 92
Milk Chocolate Toffee Bars, 99
Molasses Crinkles, 100
Peanut Butter Surprise Cookies, 93
Quick Oatmeal Cookies, 94
Yellowframe Farm Cookies, 93

CUSTARDS & PUDDINGS
Custard Bread Pudding, 126
Eartha Morrison's Chocolate Chip Dessert, 109
Easy Dirt Dessert, 109

DIPS & SPREADS
Black Bean Dip, 145
Black Bean Salsa, 13
Grandmother's Pear Chutney, 44
Guacamole, 12
Hawfields Cranberry Chutney, 44
Mandy's Mayo, 49
Pimiento Cheese, 146
Red Dip Salsa, 13
Yummy Chicken Dip, 15

FISH
15-Minute Whitefish, 71
Baked Fish, 71
Salmon with Honey Mustard Sauce, 72

FROZEN DESSERTS
Buttermilk Ice Cream, 127
Sugar Free Frozen Custard, 127

FRUIT
Curried Fruit Bake, 56
Fruit Flan, 103
Old Fashioned Honey Sauce on Fruit, 104
Sunny's Fruit Dip, 104

GRAINS & BEANS
California Rice Casserole, 52
Cowboy Beans, 59
Grittman Family Rice Consommé, 52

LAMB
Moroccan Lamb Tagine, 88

Index

PASTA
Delicious Macaroni and Cheese, 56
Fettuccine Alfredo, 87
Mac and Cheese . . . the Best Ever!, 57

PIES & PASTRIES
All Star Tartlets, 106
Apple Brown Betty, 106
Barbara (Harvey) Mentz's Blueberry Nectar Pie, 123
Blackberry Cobbler, 107
Bob Little's Favorite Pumpkin Pie with a Healthy Non Bullet-Proof Crust, 121
Chocolate Irish Coffee Mousse, 108
Chocolate Pot de Créme, 108
Chocolate Tart, 107
Deep Dish Pear Pie, 122
Kerstin's Apple Delight, 105
Lanier's Apple Crumb Pie, 123
LaVerne Harvey's Old Fashioned Apple Cream Pie, 124
Meme's Pecan Pie, 126
My Mother's Deep Dish Apple Pie, 125
Orange Blossoms, 103
Pineapple Casserole, 105
Shaker Lemon Pie, 119

PORK
Ham Biscuits, 149
Irene's Opening Meet Sausage Balls, 18
Opening Meet Hunt Breakfast Glazed Ham, 138
Pork Tenderloin with Honey Mustard and Orange Slices, 89
Sausage Stuffed Mushroom Caps, 59

POULTRY
Aunt Kitty's Doves, 68
Catherine's Chicken Piccata, 63
Charlotte Wentworth Harvey's Canadian Goose, 62
Emeline Harvey's Sunday Chicken Dinner, 65
Javanese Rice Taffle (7 Boy Curry), 66
Maggie Price's Chicken, 64
Mimomma's Yummy Chicken, 67
Picnic Chicken, 148
Sand Chicken, 63
The Easiest Slow Cooker Chicken Ever, 64
Turkey Meatloaf, 67
Wild Duck with Orange Sauce, 68

SALAD
Ann M. Boland's Tuna Fish Salad, 33
Baba's Cranberry Salad, 36
Broccoli Floret Salad, 147
Caesar Salad, 39
Cucumber Sour Cream Salad, 34
Finnish Beet Salad, 34
Fruit Salad, 36
Irene Greenberg's Strawberry Spinach Salad, 35
Marinated Kale Salad with Gouda and Apples, 35
Mom's Crab Salad, 37
Mom's Pasta Salad, 38
Shawna Smith's Chicken Salad, 31
Tuna Macaroni Salad, 38
Vermicelli Vinaigrette, 39
Wisconsin Chicken, Cranberry and Wild Rice Salad, 32
Zippy Corn Salad, 37

SHELLFISH
Baked Clams, 14
Roasted Shrimp and Guacamole, 14
Easy Crab Dip, 15
Damian and Jose's Oysters Argentina, 11
Howe Family Holiday Oysters, 70
Mrs. Martin's Curried Shrimp in Avocado Halves, 47
Spicy Shrimp Curry, 72
Shrimp with Feta, 73
Shrimp and Mango Wraps, 146
Stuffed Lobster, 70

SOUP & STEW
Backstretch Beef Stock, 23
Cowboy Stew, 75
Cowpuncher Stew, 74
Cucumber Soup, 29
Chilled Watermelon Soup, 29
Easy Slow Cooker Potato Soup, 26
Gazpacho Blanco, 30
Gazpacho, 30
Greek Beef Stew with Onions, 76
Greek Lemon Soup, 24
Irina's Borscht, 22
Liner Chili, 77
Moma's Cream of Artichoke Soup, 26
Quick Beef Stew, 75
Reflections Farm Squash Soup, 27
Ruth Hanna Strong's Squash and Sweet Potato Soup, 25
Shawna Smith's Fresh Tomato Herb Soup, 24
Taco Soup, 28
Warm Your Heart Friendship Soup, 27
Zuppa Matta, 22

VEAL
Osso Buco, 87

VEGETABLES
Aretha Fuller's Squash Casserole, 50
Asparagus Parmesan, 48
Baked Vidalia Onions, 53
Corn Pudding, 42
Herbed Yogurt Baked Tomatoes, 43
Holiday Asparagus, 48
Kickin' Cucumber Salad, 54
Kitty Walsh's Irish Potato Stuffing, 46
Moore County Potato Salad, 54
Mrs. Ellison McKissick Jr.'s Broccoli Soufflé, 58
Potato Hash Cake, 144
Red Onion Salad, 53
Spaghetti-less Spaghetti, 51
Spinach and Artichoke Casserole, 50
Sweet Potato Delight, 45
Sweet Potato Soufflé, 45
Tomato Pudding, 43
Youngs Road Scalloped Cheese Potatoes, 47

VENISON
Elk Burgers, 86
Mary Elsner Mielke's Mince Meat, 110

Thank You

Most Moore County locals are familiar with the area's classically beautiful aesthetics – from its tall pines to the pristine Walthour-Moss Foundation, our region's enchantment is undeniable. When picturing horse country, I'm reminded of the cascading ancient pines, lolling grassy pastures, and smiling faces of local horseback riders that give the area its character. Perhaps one of the more unexpected, yet delightful secrets I've discovered about the area is that it's also home to a diverse collection of talented cooks and chefs.

I want to thank everyone for joining me in the process of discovering the hidden gems of our horse country community. I've truly enjoyed the participation of all the foundation's friends, and being enriched by the character of the land displayed by its residents' unique cuisine. Thank you to all the folks who have contributed their personal flavor to the richness of **Horse Country Cooking**.

I'd like to give a special thank you to popular rider Katie Walsh. She has been the driving force of setting **Horse Country Cooking** in motion and has made publishing this cookbook easy. Her role in gathering and collecting recipes from the people who make this place home was invaluable to the heart of this book and reflects the true spirit of our community.

I also want to thank my wonderful staff for making the cookbook possible and bringing to life the picture of horse country I hold so dear. I believe we've truly captured the essence of the community we're all so fond of.

Lastly, thank you to the community for making me proud to call this place home. Just like James Taylor has "gone to Carolina" in his mind, I'll forever be gone to Southern Pines "horse country" in mine.

Best wishes and happy cooking,

Kathy Virtue

Kathy Virtue
Publisher